100%
Commission Brokerage and Death of the Big Box Realty

Published by 99 Pages or Less Publishing, LLC
Miami, FL
www.99pagesorless.com

For bulk discounts email:
info@99pagesorless.com

Cover design by: 2Faced Design

Printed in the United States of America.
10 9 8 7 6 5 4 3 2 1

Library of Congress Control Number: 2015909756
ISBN 13: 978-1-943684-00-7

Disclaimer: This publication is designed to educate, entertain, and provide some general information regarding the process of the 100% commission real-estate brokerage model. It is not meant to provide legal advice. Laws and practices often vary from state to state and are subject to change. Therefore, the reader should consult with his or her own attorney or competent professional advisor before venturing into the 100% commission real-estate brokerage model.

Every effort has been made to make this manual as complete and as accurate as possible. However, there may be some typographical mistakes and errors in content. Neither the authors nor the publisher assumes any responsibility for any errors or omissions. Furthermore, the authors and the publishers shall have neither liability nor responsibility to any person or entity with respect to any loss or damage caused, or alleged to have been caused, directly or indirectly, by the information contained in this book.

Dedication

To the smart entrepreneur who
embraces change and seizes the opportunity,
this book is for you. Thank you.

"Change, before you have to."

—JACK WELCH

100%
Commission Brokerage and Death of the Big Box Realty

Everything you need to know in 99 pages or less®

ARAM SHAH

Other Books by Aram Shah

*Reo Boom: How to Manage, List, and Cash
In on Bank-Owned Properties*

*The Art of Wholesaling Properties: How to Buy
and Sell Real Estate without Cash or Credit*

———————

For questions, comments, to learn about our
one-on-one business coaching or to download free forms
to help you grow your real-estate business please visit:

100PERCENTREALESTATE.COM

Contents

Introduction   ix

1. The Death of Big Box Realties   1

2. The Truth About 100% Commission   8

3. How 100-Percenters Recruit   16

4. How to Start a 100% Commission Brokerage   21

5. The Secret Sauce: Creating the Value Add   32

6. How to Recruit 1,000 Agents in 36 Months   40

7. Making Seven Streams of Income With 100% Commission   56

8. How Agents Can Double-Dip on Listings and Buyer Leads   68

9. Final Thoughts: For Agents, Brokers, and Buyers   75

Appendix A: Real-Estate Resources   77

Appendix B: Live-Agent Closing Script   80

Appendix C: Recruiting Ads   84

Appendix D: Rebate Agreement   86

About the Author   89

Introduction

I n 2005 I started my first real-estate brokerage firm out of the back room in my parents' house in Miami, Florida. I had no startup capital, no resources, and very little experience. I was twenty-five years old at the time, had just passed my broker exam, and realized that I wanted a piece of the Miami market. Ten years later I built one of the largest brokerage business in Florida, with over 500 sales associates, and created a stream of steady cash flow averaging $50,000 a month, while working only five hours a week, and I eventually sold it all off in 2015. All of this was accomplished by creating a niche in the marketplace with the 100% commission brokerage model.

Real-estate brokerage is an underdog business, especially for an independent, or "indie," company starting off; no one sees you coming. The key to my selling off my company and building a resilient sales force was doing something that no one else did—giving all the money back to my agents, minus a small flat fee per transaction. It was incredible. In fact, no one would believe the amount of money that could be made. It was an incredible win-win situation.

My agents would keep 100% of their commission, thus making more revenue than they would hanging their licenses next to that of a traditional real-estate broker, and I would keep a small flat fee for myself. Eventually I noticed a direct correlation between more agents and more income. While my competition (the traditional, non-100% brokers—basically everyone else in the market) was struggling to stay afloat with their intense overhead (franchise fees, lavish offices, hefty salaries, etc.), I managed to sweep up market share.

Since there was no blueprint for this brokering model, I experienced a lot of trial and error, and as a result I lost a lot of money in opportunity costs. Instead of placing my income in proven investments such as cash-flow properties, I kept it in the brokerage, not knowing what could happen. It was a steep learning curve. However, in the end I learned the art of building a brokerage and providing exceptional value to my agents. Everyone was happy and the marketplace rewarded that with dollars and cents.

This book is the revelation of my journey and methods to building a 100% commission brokerage company. All real-estate professionals, real-estate agents, brokers, investors, and homebuyers will find value in the upcoming pages because the model applies to every party.

If you are a real-estate agent who is not on this 100% commission agent-centric model, then read this book cover to cover with an open mind. It will help you save thousands of dollars in commissions lost, which means that, ultimately, you will make thousands more. If you are currently a real-estate agent who is with a 100% commission broker, read this book with the goal of understanding how the broker makes money, so that you can decide whether or not your broker is the right fit for your needs.

Finally, if you are a new or seasoned real-estate broker who is struggling to make profits or wants to boost your revenue, then heed the principles in this book—they will work wonders. Homebuyers and investors can also benefit by knowing whether or not their agent is on a 100% commission plan, because many 100% commission agents offer rebates to their customers from their commission (i.e., they pay you to buy or sell).

Real estate has always been a passion for me, and my love for the game has enabled me to constantly improve the industry by giving back. My first book, *REO Boom: How to Manage, List, and Cash in on Bank-Owned Properties* shared the secrets on real-estate-owned properties (REOs), while my other book *The Art of Wholesaling Properties: How to Buy and Sell Real Estate without Cash or Credit* gave away the insider tips on flipping real-estate contracts with no cash or credit. I hope this book reaches all the real-estate players in the marketplace who want to see financial change and improvement in their lives. My goal is to do so within 99 pages or less. So, buckle your seatbelts and let's get started!

ARAM SHAH
@SHAHOFMIAMI (Twitter/Instagram)

1

The Death of Big Box Realties

A long time ago, brokerage firms, or realties, used to charge their agents 50% of every single purchase and transaction. If the agent closed a deal and made $3,000 in gross commission, the brokerage firm would take $1,500 off the top. This "brokerage-centric model" was justified due to the lack of technology and speed of information in the marketplace. There was no Zillow.com to give free home values, no syndication of online listings, no flat-fee listings, no virtual offices, and surely no 100% commission brokerage companies—just plain old brick-and-mortar shops. One shop became two, two became four, and the rest is history, giving way to Re/Max, Century 21 Real Estate, Coldwell Banker Real Estate, Better Homes and Gardens, Keller Williams Realty, and hundreds of real-estate franchises or "big box realties" across the country.

The brokers controlled the inventory, provided the office space, and generated the buyer and seller "leads" to hand off to their top, most seasoned sales associates. Everybody wanted the "hot leads," but hated the 50% cut in pay. There was no alternative, since the broker was the boss. This model ran rampant up until the mid-1980s, when more real-estate agents entered the marketplace, along with non-franchised or "independent" brokerages. This additional supply of brokerage services led to aggressive brokerage/commission

1

agent payouts: 70/30 and 80/20 splits. There were more brokerages fighting for the same agents. So brokers had to offer a better compensation plan than did the big box realty franchises.

The agent would keep 70% or 80% of the commission they produced and the broker would keep the rest. Slowly the broker/owners realized there were diminishing returns in "franchise names" and they were simply not worth the expense. With the higher payouts to agents and hefty franchise fees, there was little room left to make any money. In fact, the top reasons why brokers and agents went independent were:

1. They did not want to pay the franchise fee (typically 6% off the gross commission and 2% for advertising [a hefty 8% from the top]).
2. They wanted to brand themselves, not someone else's company. After all, when they didn't renew the franchise agreement they stood to lose all the goodwill (contacts, leads, systems, etc.).
3. They had conflicting views with the franchisor, who only cared about opening up more shops (growth) and collecting more fees.
4. They had little to no control. Advertising, protocol, and standard operating procedures had to go through reams of red tape for approval.
5. There was no additional added value. The costs did not outweigh the benefit.

Today the numbers for franchise versus non-franchise firms tell the story—big box realty franchises are disappearing. According to the National Association of Realtors' 2014 Profile of Real Estate Firms,[1] 134,108 Realtors® were given an online survey, to which

---

1. http://www.realtor.org/news-releases/2014/10/
real-estate-firms-optimistic-about-future-of-industry.

7,081 responded. The results: 84% of real-estate firms are independent, 14% are independent franchise firms, and the remaining 2% are divided equally between subsidiaries of a national and regional corporation, both franchised and non-franchised firms.

The old-school big box realty franchises are dying. Agents don't want to work harder anymore; they want to work smarter. They don't need the corner offices and lukewarm leads; they can generate leads themselves with the targeted social media outlets, advertising opportunities such as Facebook or Realtor.com.

Even some non-franchised independent companies offer their agents only 50–60% commission and some agents are comfortable paying it, with the misconception of that being the only way to "learn" the business. These generally are the five to ten broker-agent shops with strong "hand-holding" or training from the brokers, which prevents them from scaling up and growing due to the intense time involved in nurturing their sales associates.

So why give up 50%, 60%, 70%, 80%, 90%, or even 99% of their hard-earned commission to their broker? Although the 100% commission model might not be for all agents, I argue that it *should be* due to the advancement of social media and technology that allows every broker to achieve competitive pricing and service offerings similar to the big box realty players.

Proponents of the big box, broker-centric models argue that the 100% commission firms offer no support or training, but there is insufficient evidence to back up these assertions. Some propaganda techniques I have seen include brainwashing the prospective real-estate agent at the time of education (i.e., real-estate school) to "look out" for the 100% commission brokers trying to recruit them, for their supposed lack of value-added propositions. I don't blame them for trying, but it's very difficult to compete against price.

If you're buying Product A, which offers exactly the same features as another product, Product B, but Product A is cheaper—why would you *not* choose Product A? The only way to compete is to throw Product A "under the bus." This, unfortunately, is the last resort for big box realties to stay alive, so they're often quick to bad-mouth the 100% commission broker model.

The marketplace is fierce. Big box realties have it tough with long franchise commitments, six to eight percent of every dollar going off the top to someone else's brand, no individual autonomy, and fierce competition. From 2010 to 2015, I recruited dozens of large franchise agents, who repeatedly told me that they have to pay enormous fees from their own transactions that they generated themselves. Brokers pass along the six percent to their agents, then allot their 70/30 or 80/20 split, and then they take their transaction fee, then their monthly fee, and then their technology fee. At the end of the day, the agent is left with, at most, 50% of their initial income.

The big box realty franchises, unfortunately, have to operate like this because they are vested. How else could you justify 50% of net to the agent and to the brokerage without the lavish office, lead generation, corporate trainings, and salaried employees? It's a "lose-lose" scenario, which can often cause both the real-estate agent and the broker/owner to hang up the shingle and call it quits.

Therefore, the only thing which these companies can do is to sell the vision the old way using "smoke and mirrors," which includes dozens of pep rallies, guest speakers, hand-holding seminars, networking shindigs, everything to keep the glue sticking to both sides of the puzzle. Unfortunately, within the first year of their employment, the rookie agents often get caught up in the hype, or the "upsell," but eventually seek alternative solutions, while 100% brokers sit back and wait to catch the demand of agents as they re-enter the employment marketplace. Sooner or later, many agents simply get tired of seeing their hard-earned income lining the pockets of their big box franchise, so they begin to search for a lower-cost alternative—the 100-percenters. This, in a nutshell, is the real-estate brokerage game across most markets, in most cities.

On January 5, 2015, Inman.com, a market leader in real-estate news, did a survey of 777 independent brokers and real-estate professionals, and compiled their findings in a special report entitled "The shift towards independent brokerages."[2] This report found further validating evidence regarding why the big box realties are slowly dying. What follows is a sampling of the questions and responses given.

When asked, "Why aren't you currently affiliated with a franchise brand?" over 90% chose "Didn't see the value" as a response. When asked, "Independent brokerages are on the rise. Why do you think that is?" over 60% of those questioned selected "Sense of Ownership" as a response. Another important question asked was "Who distributes more leads to their agents?" Over 60% selected the response "independents" versus selecting "franchises," which only received 36.71% of the vote.[3]

In summary, the Inman.com survey responses emphasized several reasons why independents are thriving: the ability to personalize and brand online, the customizing of services to the end consumers buying or selling their homes, independent control, less bureaucracy and politics, freedom to build one's own culture and becoming organic, and seeing no value in monthly franchise fees, to name a few. Now, combine independent brokerages with 100% commission and you have a powerhouse model ready to turn into a cash machine.

This is the new wave of real-estate brokerage. The early-adopter brokers who switch to this model will become millionaires if they grow their business by following the principles outlined in this book. The agents who recognize these changing dynamics and embrace them will earn up to 50% more in commissions. Finally, the savvy home-buyers and investors who recognize how brokers and agents work will realize that they will want to work with a 100% commission agent, as

2. http://www.inman.com/2015/01/05/
   special-report-the-shift-toward-independent-brokerages/.
3. Ibid.

these agents have the power to give them cash rebates from their commissions. The pie is big enough to divide many ways.

Conversely, those who are stubborn and set in their ways will see their business trickle down to nothing. Welcome to the world of 100% commission brokerage.

Chapter 1
POINTS TO REMEMBER

» The brokerage-centric model is the old-school model, offering low commission splits to the agent, with the broker controlling every aspect of the business.

» The agent-centric model is the newer way of making money in real estate; it empowers agents to keep most, if not all, of their pay, and puts them in the driver's seat.

» Big box realties are dying out because of the high franchise fees and overhead, rigid red tape and control, conflicting goals, and lack of customization and individual branding.

» Big box realty franchises are too heavily vested to change their brokerage model to one of 100% commission, and are therefore forced to upsell, using "smoke and mirrors" to stay afloat.

» There's immense opportunity for both brokers and agents to embrace the 100% commission model to achieve greater financial success by keeping more money in each of their pockets.

2

The Truth about
100% Commission

So, is 100% commission really 100%, or is it too good to be true? Yes. Well, sort of. Allow me to explain. The typical structure of the 100% brokerage model involves the broker giving their agent all of the commission earned (i.e., 100%), less a small flat fee per transaction. Some 100% brokerages, or "100-percenters," charge their agents monthly fees on top of the flat fee, and almost all charge an errors and omissions (E&O) insurance fee (to defend against lawsuits), as well as a nominal transaction fee (e.g., $395) at the time the transaction closes. This transaction fee is customary throughout the industry, from the small 100-percenter to the largest big box realty franchise. Many buyers and sellers consider this a "junk fee" because it really doesn't have anything to do with assistance with selling or buying a home.

Here's how all brokerages perceive it. This transaction fee is charged to the agent by the broker. Usually, the agent tries to pass this fee along to their client (seller or buyer). If the client does not want to pay this transaction fee (which is usually the case, as everything is negotiable), the agent ends up paying for it. Many times agents will justify this nominal flat fee because they are discounting their services to the buyer or seller (for example, an agent could take a listing at a four-percent fee versus the customary six percent, or offer a $2,000 cash rebate to purchase a property, less the flat fee). Another way they justify it is by saying that a portion goes to a "transaction coordinator in the office" to manage the paperwork.

Regardless, if the client refuses to pay then the agent has to pay, as it's usually mandated by the broker (i.e., company policy). However, an agent is not going to lose a customer for a couple hundred bucks! As a result, this fee is received by all brokerages, both 100-percenters and big box realties.

Therefore, the four guaranteed ways a 100-percenter makes money directly on each of its agents' transactions are as follows:

1. A flat fee per transaction (typically $199–$995)
2. An E&O insurance fee per transaction (typically $50–$250)
3. A transaction fee for either the buyer or the seller (typically $199–$699)
4. A monthly fee (typically $49–$399) with a lower or zero transaction fee.

There are also multiple streams of hidden income that the broker makes off of each file, which we will cover in chapter seven. For now, let's throw some numbers behind this scenario. Let's assume a $250,000 sales price and the agent makes 3%. In the 100% scenario, the agent's gross = $250,000 x 0.03, which comes out to $7,500.

So what's the difference? If an agent were employed with a big box realty franchise, the typical commission split for a rookie agent (an agent with one or two years' experience in the business) would be as follows:

AGENT NET WITH A BIG BOX REALTY FRANCHISE

$250,000 PP x 3% commission = $7,500 gross commission to agent

- » Less 6% franchise fee: $450
- » Less transaction fee (yes, they also have them): $299
- » Less technology fee: $50

$6,701 off the top, now *less* the applicable big box realties' commission split fees (depending on the contract between broker and agent):

Less: 60/40 split model

Broker taking 40% from agent: $2,680.40
Agent keeps only 60%: $4,020.60

Less: 70/30 split model

Broker taking 30% from agent: $2,010.30
Agent keeps only 70%: $4,690.70

Less: 80/20 split model

Broker taking 20% from agent: $1,340.20
Agent keeps only 80%: $5,360.80

These big box realty splits are dependent on the firm's policies, but are customary across most companies. This, of course, assumes no monthly fee, which many big box realties also charge (typically ranging from $59 to $595 a month). Even at an 80/20 split, the agent only keeps 20%, or $5,360.80, in his or her pocket. Compare that to a 100% commission outfit with no monthly fees:

AGENT NET WITH A 100% BROKERAGE

$250,000 PP x 3% commission = $7,500 gross commission to agent

- » Less flat fee: $300
- » Less transaction fee: $395
- » Less E&O insurance: $100

(Total of a $795 "all-in" flat fee)

100% Commission Split Agent Net: $6,705.00

vs.

80/20 Big Box Realty Net to Agent: $5,360.80

=

$1,344.20 in savings by joining a 100-percenter!

There is no question that 100% commission puts more money back in the agent's pockets. This holds true especially for the higher-purchase properties that the agent sells.

Imagine a $1,000,000-plus luxury home or condo in dense, hot markets such as Miami, San Diego, or New York City:

$1 million x 3% sales commission = $30,000
Less the all-in flat fee of $795
= a net of $29,205 to the agent!

Imagine giving 20% of your hard-earned $30,000 commission to your broker (i.e., $6,000). It just doesn't make business sense to hang your shingle with a non-100-percenter.

Okay, so what's the catch? Here it is. Ready? On the really lower-end homes (and this is what most, if not all, 100% brokers won't tell you when recruiting an agent), it's practically the same net effective commission split as that of a big box realty franchise. Let's redo the math with a hypothetical purchase price of $75,000 this time:

AGENT NET WITH A BIG BOX REALTY

$75,000 PP x 3% commission = $2,250 gross commission to agent

- Less 6% franchise fee: $135
- Less transaction fee (yes, they also have them): $249
- Less technology fee: $50

That's $1,816 off the top, now less:

Less: 60/40 split model

Broker taking 40% from agent: $726.40
Agent keeps only 60%: $1,089.60

Less: 70/30 split model

Broker takes 30% from agent: $544.80
Agent keeps only 70%: $1,271.20

Less: 80/20 split model

Broker takes 20% from agent: $363.20
Agent keeps only 80%: $1,452.80

(All three payouts are still under a 100% brokerage structure.)

AGENT NET WITH A 100% BROKERAGE

$75,000 PP x 3% commission = $2,250 gross commission to agent

- » Less flat fee: $300
- » Less transaction fee: $395
- » Less E&O insurance: $100

(Total $795 "all-in" flat fee)

100% commission agent net: $1,455.00

Real commission split: $1,455/$2,250 gross commission = ~65%

Even though the 100% commission split ends up being about 65% net to the agent, it still pays slightly more (in our example it pays three dollars more) than a traditional big box realty model. At the end of the day, you should care about what's in your pocket (net), not the paper percentage that it yields.

Also, one more thing: if an agent is choosing which customer to work with, one who wants to buy a $75,000 home or one who wants to buy a $175,000 home, they would probably choose the latter—it pays more. Also, it takes the same amount of time and effort to handle a $75,000 transaction or, thinking big, a $1,750,000 transaction. You still have to schedule appointments, drive buyers around, open up escrow, write contracts, do inspections, etc.

Alternatively, what is the likelihood that your market has these lower-priced homes (under $75,000)? They are few and far between. According to RealtyTrac.com, the United States's median selling price as of April 2015 was $192,000.[4] Therefore, since an agent values his or her time, it pays (literally) to do business with a 100% commission brokerage company, especially for properties with higher purchase prices.

---

4 http://www.realtytrac.com/statsandtrends.

Chapter 2
POINTS TO REMEMBER

» One-hundred-percent-commission structures pay out more and put more money back in the agent's pocket than do big box realty franchises' commission splits.

» A 100% broker can make money directly from their agents in four different ways: by charging a flat fee per transaction, by charging for E&O insurance, by charging a buyer or seller transaction fee, and sometimes by charging a monthly fee to offset a higher flat-fee charge.

» When the median sales price dips below $75,000, the 100% commission payout still pays slightly more than that of big box realty franchises, but the net commission split paid to the agent is practically the same.

3

How 100-Percenters Recruit

ecruiting is at the heart of brokerage. To create a resilient brokerage company that can yield you a steady stream of passive income, you have to recruit agents by the dozens. A broker's role is to recruit sales agents, while an agent's role is to represent clients (both sellers and buyers). Depending on state law, a licensed sales associate or agent is required to hang their license with a broker for certain period of time. For some states, this period is as little as one year, while, for others, it's as long as five years.

At my firm our philosophy was "If they are licensed and breathing, they are in." We took anyone. Zero experience? No problem. Been in the game for thirty years? Even better. Obviously, the goal was to find the seasoned agents, but we discovered after ten years of recruiting that the seasoned agents were very difficult to convert. They were in too deep. Too many trophies on the wall, too much edification, and they ran the treadmill so long and hard they were privileged to be given a "high" 90% commission split at best.

The easiest agents to bring on board were the ones who "drank the Kool-Aid" at the big box realty franchises for a year or so, got some experience at the expense of the exhaustive and elaborate "training" programs of the competition, and were ready for change. Money was the motivation; they kept their eyes on the prize and we kept our eyes on them.

A 100% broker's key to success is recruiting, recruiting, recruiting. When you are a 100% broker you are selling on price. If you're the best deal in town, agents will call you to inquire about joining your firm. Remember: you are offering the agent 100% of their earnings and keeping only a flat fee per transaction. If you get a lead that finds you, it's a godsend. We call that a "warm lead." They either find you through your online marketing, word of mouth, or a referral. We'll touch on the art of recruiting by the hundreds in a subsequent chapter. Right now, understand that the primary objective of a 100% commission broker is to get the agent into the office.

In my firm of 500-plus agents we had a mantra—ABC: Always Be Closing. Anyone in sales knows that nothing matters until the transaction closes and, in our case, the real-estate agent signing up was the transaction. Our mission was to add volume with supersonic speed.

The four biggest milestones that any new 100% broker needs to hit are: recruiting 50 agents, recruiting 100 agents, recruiting 200 agents, and recruiting 300 agents. Once a brokerage can build an agent base past 300 agents, it's put on autopilot. It's a giant, large-value network feeding itself automatically: agents bringing in more agents, who bring in more transactions, who keep more money in their pockets, which, in turn, leads to referring more agents.

When a real-estate agent passes their exam and is seeking employment, they are solicited by hundreds of brokers (both 100-percenters and non-100-percenters) that participate in their local marketplace. Note that within the non-100-percenters you will have the big box realty franchises. For every dollar that their agent makes, the franchisor gets a piece of the pie before anyone gets paid. Typically 6–8% off the gross commission income is sliced off the top, and thus the brokers can, at best, offer 90–94% commissions to their agents in payouts. However, remember from chapter two that the typical split is between 50% and 80% at most.

Every brokerage firm in the game (100-percenters and non-100-percenters), is going to promise an agent the same things. Here are the top six value-added propositions, in order of importance. These are the six unkept promises that each brokerage company constantly juggles to recruit and retain by the hundreds. They are considered "unkept" because it's very difficult to provide all six propositions constantly at a given time. For example, many big box realties will trade off a higher commission split to the agent for a fancy office.

In the following list, the order of importance goes from the top down for a non-100-percenter, and from the bottom up for a 100% broker:

1. Branding and Technology
2. Support
3. Office Space
4. Trainings
5. Leads
6. Higher Commissions

The big box realty franchises sell on price last and "value" first. They have the 200-year-old brand and the high-tech platform, the one-on-one support, conference rooms and cubicles for agents to use, live trainings, lead generation, and, lastly, a stair-step commission structure where the more sales you make, the more your commission increases. For example, if you are a brand-new agent, they start you at a 50% commission split and justify it with the four aforementioned propositions. Then, if you are worthy and produce sales, you get bumped up to 80, 90, or maybe, if you are the number-one sales agent in the tri-county area, 100% commission.

In contrast, the 100-percenters sell on price first. Here is a sample recruiting pitch that I use when signing up agents:

Why jump through hoops, work hard for your boss, and be forced to attend pep rallies when, from day one, whether you make one transaction or 100 transactions, you keep 100% commission, less a $199 transaction fee? Make sense? Also, let me now tell you about our lead program, and our one-on-one mentorship program, our 24-7 conference room and office, our broker support and our online platform. What's not to like? Plus there's no contract, so you can leave any time and take your listings. Why?

We don't care to keep your listings. Remember that we only make a couple hundred a file; we're not slicing up your pay and controlling you. Okay, I need a copy of your real-estate license; meanwhile, please start filling out the standard independent contractor's agreement here.

Close, close, close! It's too easy.

Of course, the 100% broker has to have the other five value-added propositions to offer other than just the 100% commission structure. When I started out I had a virtual office, paid $350 a month and secured a professional "Class A" (top shelf) office building with a shared secretary and a gorgeous conference room overlooking the bay. Agents would drop off files or upload them onto my back office site, and I would review the paperwork and pay them on the same day, less my nominal transaction fee. It worked. That was ten years ago. Today, if you are a 100% broker without the other five items, you are dead in the water.

But don't worry. If you are starting your own shop—the next chapter is for you.

Chapter 3
POINTS TO REMEMBER

» 100-percenters recruit everyone; it's a numbers game.

» 100-percenters sell on price first, as opposed to non-100-percenters, who sell on value first.

» A large value network turns into a cash machine after the four biggest milestones are achieved.

» Fulfilling the six top value-added propositions constantly is the unkept promise that every broker tries to fulfill. Those who achieve this unlock the secret to recruiting by the hundreds.

4

How to Start a 100% Commission Brokerage

I loved owning a real-estate brokerage. It was exciting. It was easy. It was fun. What I really loved about it was that anyone could do it; the barriers to entry were extremely low. At least in Florida (and in most states), no college degree is required. Pass the state exam as a sales associate, hang your license with an active broker for a couple of years (depending on which state), pass the broker exam, and you are ready to make millions! Okay, maybe not millions (initially), but surely you will make hundreds of thousands. Many of my friends who had high-volume shops were making two to three times the yearly income that the median attorney, doctor, architect, or CPA was making, and all of those careers require rigorous schooling.

The 100% commission brokerage model is a high-paced, high-volume transactional game. You have to love doing deals, as many as you can (accurately), and as fast as possible. The absolute best part of the 100% commission model is the passive income. It's like purchasing a multifamily commercial building or a small commercial office building without putting your life savings into it for the down payment, the tenant headache, the strenuous regulations, and, most importantly, a 60–70% bank loan. It's purely passive income. Every day your agent is hitting the streets, writing contracts, showing homes, preparing listing agreements, and opening up escrow, while you're in your office writing checks and paying agents. I always used to say that a business is not really passive unless you're making money while you sleep. This is the closest thing to it. Once you have a bona-fide passive income stream companies will buy you out and pay you a nice premium for it. Unless, of course, you don't want to sell.

Here's how it works. Every month, your agent closes a transaction, you get your cut (e.g., $795), and you give them the rest. Agents love it. They keep all the commissions, less your flat fee per file. You love it because they are motivated to do more deals. The customer loves it because many agents offer a portion of their commissions back as a home-buying rebate, which we will come back to later. The point is that it's an aggressive storm and once it catches steam, it just makes you more money.

In chapter two, we discussed the four *direct ways* a broker makes revenue from their agents. Here is the recap:

1. A flat fee per transaction (typically $199–$995)
2. An E&O insurance fee per transaction (typically $50–$250)
3. A buyer or seller transaction fee (or "additional commission fee") (typically $199–$699)
4. A monthly fee (typically $49–$399 a month) with a lower or zero transaction fee.

Here are the three *indirect ways* in which a broker makes money from their agents (which I will explain in more detail in chapter seven):

1. Charging a big box realty-style commission split on *leads* given out (e.g., 70/30).
2. Making money pushing their own or affiliated title and mortgage companies.
3. Commission advances and overrides.

Think of it this way. When you see a coupon in the newspaper, you clip it or download and scan it with your smartphone, and visit your nearest retailer. When you arrive at the store, the item you are going to buy is probably placed all the way in the back, or at the end of the aisles. Why? So you can walk through the store to purchase everything else. Thus, the item discounted is nothing more than a "loss-leader" and the real money is made on everything else in the middle of the aisles.

The same goes with the 100% commission brokerage. You make very little on the agents' deals, but you make full-priced margins on the indirect income. The entire business relies on volume. Now you know why the bigger firms have their "in-house" title and mortgage all in house. They pitch the "all-in-one convenience," but if you read between the lines, you will realize that the ancillary income is necessary for them to survive and grow. Once an independent firm is as big as a big box realty, they can offer the exact same value proposition or menu at half the costs. Can you blame an agent for not wanting to hang their license with a big box realty firm? That's the end goal and that's how you take market share.

We will dive into the nuts and bolts of the seven streams of income in chapter seven, but for now just keep in mind that, as a 100% brokerage, you have the ability to print money! If you are starting out as an agent who just got licensed, think about owning your own shop within the next 24 months. When I started, I went from licensed sales associate to licensed broker in 12 months. No interruptions, no experience (i.e., straight out of college). I knew what I wanted, but I didn't know the potential. I learned along the way, and wish I had had a book like this at the time. So, agents, team leaders, broker associates, and current brokers, here it is.

First things first, get your licenses out of the way, set up your LLC, and think branding. I'm not going to get into the granular "how to set up a website, S corp versus LLC, etc." I don't want to bore you with the details. Besides, I included a real-estate resource (see Appendix A) to help you find vendors to do all the things you need to do to make money.

Talk to a CPA and an attorney. Check out www.avvo.com to get free legal questions answered. Since I was in Florida, I went to my state's website to file an "Articles of Incorporation" for myself for under $150.00. Anyone in Florida can visit www.sunbiz.org to open up their own corporation or LLC.

Okay, back to the big picture. Branding is key. First, visit www.godaddy.com and see if the company domain name you are thinking about is available. You want to envision yourself running a 1,000-member team operation and all your agents having your logo, brand, and website URL on houses across the city.

Also, in the beginning it's important to think about an exit strategy before an entrance strategy. In my company I included "Florida" in the name because I knew my exit strategy was to stay regional in order to be bought out. Besides, I wanted all the real-estate agents in Florida to quickly know who we were and what we did; therefore, I also included "100% commission" in the actual name of my company.

Why? Better placement on search engines, and most importantly, on the multiple listing service, or "MLS," where every other agent could see what we were about. My theory was that they would see our name, be overcome with curiosity, and then give us a call. It worked. It made my job much easier.

Some of my clients, who were opening up their own shops, have asked me "Should I put my last name in the brokerage name?" I say that it depends. What's the holding period for which you anticipate keeping the company? Some of the biggest companies, such as Keller Williams Realty, have been around for decades. If you're looking to build a steady stream of income to sell it off quickly, I would advise against it.

Conversely, if your goal is to create a lifestyle business and keep it to pay the bills and the extracurricular family fun activities every year, and you have no intentions to sell, then go for it. Think of it like this:

if you were gone tomorrow, could someone else come in and keep it afloat? Would your potential end buyer feel comfortable buying you out and operating under your first or last name? I wouldn't. However, if the name was something neutral, like XYZ Realty, he or she could step right in and no stakeholder would know the difference.

Next is the office. Today it is a must. Ten years ago I had a very expensive website and virtual office, which I built up to fifty agents without any reservation. However, today almost every broker who has scaled his or her operation has a physical office. The good news is that since we are selling on price (i.e., 100% commission) it's justified to have an office in a "Class B or C" full-service building. This means that it's the lower-end price point of office-space leasing and the landlord takes care of all the expenses for you (air-conditioning, water, janitorial, maintenance, etc.), so all you're doing is writing a monthly check.

Other than price, the next biggest factor in choosing a location is parking. It needs to be unlimited and free. Remember that you will have hundreds of agents moving in and out, so if you are in a building where parking is a nightmare in terms of costs or convenience, real-estate agents will be turned off. If you are in a really dense area, one solution to this is finding a building next to a large supermarket or a park where agents can park and walk over to your office building. Finally, you need to think about where to locate your office. This means thinking about who your target agent really is. This depends on the target sales price. Some cities will have a wide variety of median sales prices, from $75,000 to over $7,500,000. Some will not.

Remember that this business is about volume and turn. The more transactions you can turn or "churn" out, the more money you will make. For example, in Miami, the majority of the high transactions were occurring under the $250,000 price point. There are a lot more buyers for a financeable, lower-priced property who could easily qualify for a Federal Housing Administration (FHA)-insured mortgage or conventional financing, and it can be easier to court these customers rather than relying on a million-dollar home to sell, which depends upon the buyer obtaining a "jumbo loan." Yet, every market is different. You want to make sure there are a lot of transactions happening within a specific price point, then figure out where that area of town is, and find your office to lease within it. Here was the blueprint in almost all the locations we had:

100% BLUEPRINT: LESS THAN 1500 SQUARE FEET

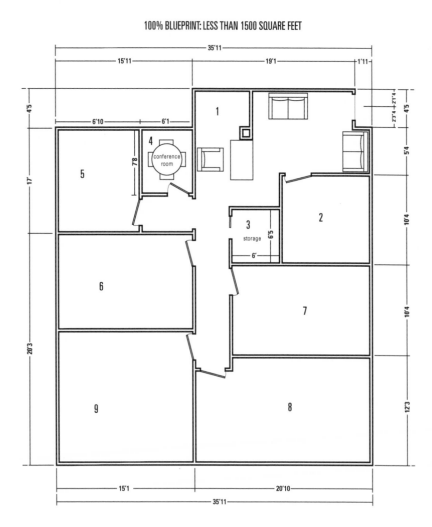

When choosing your office space, it's critical to be conservative for the first 36 months in terms of furnishings and location. In my first book, *REO Boom: How to Manage, List, and Cash in on Bank-Owned Properties*, I talk a lot about bootstrapping and using your current cash to slowly grow. I am a big advocate against debt. I just don't like it. Assuming that you're like me and your budget (working capital) is small, here is the footprint of what you should look for: an office size no greater than 1,500 square feet for $20 a square foot. Your monthly check to the landlord should be no greater than 1,500 square feet x $20 = $30,000 / 12 months = $2,500 a month.

To offset the monthly rent and size, which is attractive and sufficient to compete with the big box realty franchises, you want to have the layout designed so that it can be divided up into as many offices as possible. What you don't use, you sublet out for $300–500 a month. Here was the typical office setup, which included the five necessary partitions:

1. Receptionist
2. Recruiter room
3. Sales pit
4. Small conference table
5. Broker or office manager's office

In our office, we had a little more than the five partitions. Remember: what you don't use you can sublease out. Referring to the layout blueprint sketch on page 26, as soon as you walk in, you have your receptionist to greet you (1), followed by a sublet office in the receptionist area (2). Here customers can wait and/or chat with the subleased vendor. In the beginning, since you will not be big enough to have your "in-house" ancillary services, you want to sublease to these specific types of vendors (insurance, home inspectors, title, etc.). The minute you scale up your operations, you can take over that space. This helps you pay down that rent.

Next, your agents walk past the reception area, past the storage room (3), and then there are nothing but offices down the long corridor. Office (4) is the small conference room for your agent to use with their clients, and office (5) is the sales pit out of which your agents work. You want to have three to five cubicles in the sales pit in case your agents want to pass by and knock out some contracts or fill out some listing agreements. Office (6) or (7) can be where your recruiting team is. This is important. Remember that, initially, your receptionist will be the recruiter, but eventually you want one or two full-time recruiters "dialing for dollars," as they say in the industry. If office (6) is the recruiter, then rent out office (7) or vice versa.

Next is office (8), the training room; I had a long white board and stacked sixteen chairs in that room. This is your sizzle room. Where your future trainer (not you) teaches your agents how to make money. Finally, office (9) is where you sit, along with your office manager. Initially, whatever you don't use you're subleasing for dirt cheap, with the goal of minimizing your costs as fast as possible. From the subleased perspective, it beats having a plain old P.O. box or working out of home. Plus, you can work together with these separate vendors on specific transactions. It's a great working environment.

Another important tip is to never have your own office; rather, give your recruiter their own. You want them to be comfortable making sales pitches and closing prospects without another person sitting at a desk across from them, eavesdropping. I also shared my office with my office manager. I wanted our future agents to know that, as a principal broker, I was accessible by always having an open-door policy.

Again, I want you to keep your overhead low. Grow into your space. Don't get excited and start spending money that you do not have. Remember: only spend money from income made. Never spend more than 40% of revenue for growth. If you make $10,000 in a month, don't spend more than $4,000 to grow. You need reserves for surprises. Also, every dollar you spend you should make two dollars or more back. If you made $10,000 in a month and you have $4,000 to spend, don't spend $4,000 on a fancy conference table. Rather, spend it on some solid targeted marketing to attract more agents, such as pay-per-click ads or targeted Facebook marketing.

In the beginning, you and your receptionist will wear all the different hats. Having a receptionist is not necessary at this point. However, if you can afford it, I would highly recommend it. You can tell a startup company easily if the same person that answers all the calls is sending out all the emails, or if you call the phone and the person answering puts you on hold every two minutes to click over to another call. That's okay for now. Here they are:

Start up 100% brokerage mode:

- Receptionist: open office, answer phone calls, filter leads, set agent appointments for brokers to recruit.
- Broker: recruit and sign up agents, review contracts, coach, provide training, hand out leads, source technology to make your life easier, sell real estate (in the beginning), close office.

When I first started and saw traction with sales and agent recruiting, I got the courage to scale up the operations by signing my first office lease. I also got my first receptionist, who worked part-time. I started her at 25 hours a week for $15 an hour. Only after I saw results and validity in sales-agent growth did I increase her hours. For every dollar that you put in, there is a risk that you won't get it back. Be shrewd. Be wise. As far as paperwork goes, your local association of Realtors® will have every single contract and standardized form that you need. There's no need to start spending hundreds of dollars in monthly fees to software companies.

With that being said, you must belong to the Realtor® association. For the fee, it pays dividends. They have a monopoly on the MLS, and you and your agents will need that to list and show homes.

There's no way around it. Next comes mastering marketing. Before you turn on the lights of your newly leased office, I want you to have the firm commitments of two to three potential sublets, as well as all of your social media branding in place.

For the sublet commitments, post a few ads on craigslist.com to solicit prospects. As far as the branding goes, set up social-media accounts. Don't worry; you don't have to know how to do any of this. Simply post an ad on www.elance.com and have dirt-cheap labor from around the globe bid on the work. These four different sites are necessary to develop a powerful online presence:

1. Instagram
2. Facebook
3. Twitter
4. Your agency's own business site

Set an official launch date and work backwards. You have one chance to make a good impression, so make sure that the minute a potential agent sees you online, they are impressed with your website and social-media presence. Also, absolutely no boilerplate templates. Make sure that all your work is custom and professional.

So you have a powerful name, you have your lease, you have two or three subtenants excited to join, you have designed your office blueprint, and you have outsourced all your social media to look like that of a company that's been around for centuries. Now, how do you get the first agent in the door? This is what the next chapter is all about, and it's what I like to call "the secret sauce." Grab some water and a notepad; let's get to work.

Chapter 4
POINTS TO REMEMBER

» A 100% commission brokerage, when scaled up, is a business that makes you money while you sleep. It's truly passive income.

» A 100% commission broker's job is to get agents in the door like a grocery store "loss leader" coupon. Once they're committed, the real money is made off of the four ancillary services.

» The perfect footprint is up to 1,500 square feet at a maximum of $20 per square foot, "full service lease," with tons of opportunities to sublet offices.

» Never put more than 40% of sales back into the business. Also, make sure that every expense is a revenue-producing expense, such as targeted Facebook ads, as opposed to buying a fancy conference table.

» Make a great first impression by having all social media completed prior to your office launch, and secure firm sublet commitments from potential ancillary vendors.

5

The Secret Sauce:
Creating the Value Add

Look to your left; look to your right. In every shopping center you will find the usual suspects: grocery store, dentist, barber shop, salon, and, most likely, a real-estate brokerage office. So what makes you so special? What is your "value add"? Just selling on price (i.e., 100% commission)? Not really. In today's marketplace it's not enough to simply sell on price. Sure, you can have a decent-sized outfit with under 50 agents, but if you want to make the real bucks, you want to grow to over 300 agents. You need a secret sauce, a secret weapon to make you attract hundreds, if not thousands, of agents to your door. So what do agents want?

Well, in chapter three we discussed the six unkept promises that every brokerage tries to implement:

1. Branding and Technology
2. Support
3. Office Space
4. Trainings
5. Leads
6. Higher Commissions

With the 100% commission structure, your value advantage (i.e., "value add") is not only to fulfill these six items, but to offer something that is outside the box that no competitor can duplicate. For example, at my firm we specialized in real-estate-owned properties (REOs) and foreclosures. We represented and sold for some of the largest banks in the industry, such as Fannie Mae, Freddie Mac, HUD, Bank of America, etc. Our secret sauce was having exclusive REO inventory that could not be found in the MLS. That's right: off-market properties or, as they say in the trade, "pocket listings."

As an agent, imagine having direct access to hot REO inventory before it hits the market (MLS). Now imagine telling all your clients that you have access to that. Imagine telling your clients that your brokerage firm represents some of the largest sellers of REOs in the industry. How many clients will you get who are looking for deals? A ton. Many of my agents grew their client bases by two or three times by working our inventory.

Not only did they make 100% commission and pay a small flat fee per file, but they had exclusive access to off-market inventory. They knew the repair status on the home, whether it was vacant or occupied, estimated time to hit the market, a ballpark estimate of what it would cost, etc., before their competition (other real-estate agents) just because they belonged to our firm. In other words, they had access to the "whisper numbers," as they say on Wall Street, or inside information that no one else had. This meant that they could present inventory to their clients earlier, have their clients conduct inspections or "due diligence" faster, and have their clients drive by the property before their competition knew it was even on the market.

Therefore, what value can you add that is different and not duplicable? Here are nine winning ideas that many of my coached clients (brokers) implemented when they first opened their 100% commission brokerage:

1. Exclusive wholesale or rehab properties. (These are "distressed" properties or "fixer-uppers" that need repair and are priced below market value.)
2. Exclusive developer listings
3. An extremely lavish office
4. Concierge services to chauffer agents and their clients around
5. Paid-for advertising
6. Beautiful staff members
7. Homebuyer rebate programs
8. Commission draws
9. Assigned parking and office space

The first two focus on the supply side of the equation: listings. Can you offer your team exclusive listings that are not found on the MLS? A great way to do so is by specializing in a niche. One of my coached clients started his business wholesaling homes. In my book *The Art of Wholesaling Properties: How to Buy and Sell Real Estate without Cash or Credit*, we discuss the lucrative ways to assign contracts to cash investors who are seeking returns on their investments with very little risk, also known as "wholesaling homes." If you are a broker, you can pitch something to your agents that can help them make more money, something more than just the six unkept promises.

In addition, many people who go to "flipping houses" seminars pay thousands of dollars to learn how to make money. If you can offer this to your agents for free to as part of a workshop or seminar (custom in-house training), you can provide a value advantage that very few competitors can replicate. Remember that you don't have to do the training; you can hire an exclusive trainer who has the specialized skills and is willing to work with your brokerage on an exclusive basis.

Another approach involves having an "in" with a developer who doesn't want to do the sales aspect of the business. Their job is to simply develop and manage the construction, so they hire you exclusively to represent them as their inside sales force on the development project. This tactic works incredibly well when it comes to recruiting agents. You will have to know developers or solicit developers prior to pitching your firm. One great way of doing this is by letting them know your plans and how you will have a huge sales force with over 1,000 agents and how you plan on achieving that within 36 months (stay tuned for the next chapter) with your unique 100% commission brokerage model.

Okay, if you don't have any advantage on the listing side and you have a little bit of spending money, then you can certainly "flex" by having a fancy office. One broker with whom I consulted started out from day one with an idea to have a 3,300-square-foot office overlooking the river with unlimited parking. His motto was that if his non-100% commission broker competitors are giving their agents half the size and charging them 30 or 40% on each deal, then his bankroll can give him a competitive advantage.

He not only had a lavish office, but he combined this with billboard advertising in his city. Within six months, he grew his agent base by 300 agents. Money talks. One caveat about this method is that it may not be sustainable in the long run because you can replicate it. If your value advantage is only having a bigger budget or bankroll, your competition can take you out of business if their bankroll is larger than yours. They can do more advertising, hire more recruiters, drop their price or flat fee, and go through a price war with you. Use this strategy only as a short-term fix if need be.

How about offering all your agents free limo services for their showings? Okay, maybe not limos, but how about a Cadillac Escalade with chauffeurs at certain times during the day? This works great in dense cities where parking is an issue. Again, if you have the bankroll, think bigger—like a Bentley or a Rolls Royce. Remember: you don't always have to buy the cars; you can lease them if the numbers work. This falls under the heavy bankroll bucket and is a unique way to truncate your competitors' reach.

Next comes paying for ads in local papers for your agents' listings. For example, buying an interior spread in a commonly read magazine and putting in 10–15 listings for any agent that has over 10 listings. Every month you can feature their listings without a cost to them, while incentivizing them to work hard to make the spread. This can also be done with online advertising via direct pay-per-click advertising on Facebook or search engines.

Another classic is beauty. One of my clients did extremely well by hiring mostly beautiful men and women as staff (not agents). His target was the younger crowd and he wanted to appeal to that agent base. Almost everyone was young, beautiful, and hip, and every time you walked into that office it was like walking into a nightclub. Plus, every three months they would literally throw large parties with a lot of food and liquor (open bar) for their associates. Then they would take hundreds of pictures and blast it all over social media. By the time the first quarter's party was up, the next one was coming. Repeat. Everyone wanted to be part of that brokerage. In this case, 100% commission and quarterly parties plus beautiful people equaled a winning situation.

As the old adage says, "Sex sells." Think about it. If everyone were offering the same menu would you hang your license with the firm with beautiful staff or the one with not-so-beautiful staff? Beauty is in the eye of the beholder, right? If you go this route, try hiring from a modeling agency. They have a lot of younger, cheaper labor looking to get their big break in acting or modeling who are willing to work part-time in an office (or try recruiting a bartender). Of course, they should be qualified to perform their assigned tasks, so don't just hire someone because they look attractive. Also remember: don't discriminate, and consult with an attorney if in doubt.

Next, focus on the demand side of the equation via homebuyer cash rebates. If your company policy is to require your agents to offer everyone who buys a home a rebate of 20–30% off their commission they earn, then your agent's retention of that client will skyrocket and they will, in turn, do more business, and refer more business. It doesn't always have to be cash: a free 50" LED TV, furniture, interior designer services, anything that is substantial in value works wonders with the 100% commission model. Why? Because there's room in the pie to divide.

Compare this to a big box realty franchise. If, after your broker chops your hard-earned pay down to 50% net, how can you then give another 30% to your homebuyer? It's not worth it for you. Thus, another buyer lost to a 100-percenter. However, if you are on a 100% commission plan, after your flat fee per transaction, you can offer your homebuyer a cash rebate to purchase. This is a great advantage, as you are helping homebuyers with closing costs or making their home-buying dreams come true.

Sometimes they just need a little extra cash to own a home. Just make sure to check with your local state laws or ask an attorney prior to doing this to ensure that it is legal (in some states it may not be). Two big brokerages that are known for this are Redfin and Zip Realty. Too bad they don't offer 100% commission to their agents.

Another strategy is to offer your agents a commission advance. The minute they lock up a contract on their home and are past the due diligence period (i.e., their buyer's money is nonrefundable or "hard"), you can advance them a portion of their commission. You can even charge them a fee of 10–15% for that service. Tons of real-estate agents need money today and as long as you are cheaper than a check-cashing store, you can make magic happen and create a win-win situation.

Finally, we have assigned parking, or an assigned office space. Ever walk into a bank and notice how everyone is "Vice President" of something? Funny how they all have vice-president titles, but their salaries are not equivalent. This is the old management technique of stroking egos. Money is not always the number-one motivation. Sometimes it's a pat on the back, a $20 trophy, a plug at the end-of-the-year party, a fancy title, an assigned parking spot or office space. In sum, it's more than the unkept promises (i.e., price and value) that brings agents on board. It's an added value, a missing piece of the puzzle, a secret sauce that no one can replicate. This is how the professionals grow brokerages.

Chapter 5
POINTS TO REMEMBER

» To grow to 300-plus agents, supplying the unkept promises is not sufficient. You need the value-added "secret sauce" to grow exponentially.

» Value-added service is something you can provide that is different and cannot be duplicated.

» Examples of value-added services are focusing on the supply side and getting exclusive off-market listings, focusing on your bankroll and offering concierge services or lavish offices, or focusing on the demand side and offering home rebates.

6

How to Recruit 1,000 Agents in 36 Months

One word: Chipotle. If you have not been to one, go. They move customers faster than the speed of light through that fast-food joint, just like what you need to do with your 100% brokerage shop. The secret in recruiting hundreds, if not thousands, is creating an assembly line of services and support. The 100% commission model is about getting hundreds of agents to sign up by any means necessary. Before big box realty franchises cringe at that last statement, know that there is a very precise way of managing risk while recruiting the masses.

But first, here's how to start. The good news about the real-estate brokerage industry is that there are a lot of free data from which you can pull. For example, in Florida you can request from the Department of Business and Professional Regulation (www.myfloridalicense.com) a list of every single real-estate agent and broker within your zip code, city, county, or even state. They provide you with names, numbers, mailing addresses, email addresses, and more. Alternatively, using the MLS, you can also search under brokerage offices and see who the brokers and the agents are. The top five ways to recruit using the 100% commission model are:

1. Calls "dialing for dollars"
2. Online targeted ads and email blasts
3. Direct mail to new licensees
4. Social-media blasts
5. Referrals from existing agents.

First, and the most important, are outbound calls. These are your bread and butter. Your job as a 100% broker is to call every single real-estate agent in town and let them know that you exist. Believe me: agents are tired of giving away their hard-earned pay to their brokers. In fact, many think it's too good to be true, but that is what makes them curious and gets them in the door when you are asking for the appointment.

Your part-time receptionist (in the beginning) or your full-time recruiter's job is to make phone calls and set appointments for you. Their sole purpose is to get agents in the door. The art in closing appointments on the phone has to do with what not to tell the agents. You cannot tell them too much; rather, tell them just enough to get them curious. Remember the value-add formula from the previous chapter? Here is a sample script showing how you can incorporate that:

Hello, John, this is YOUR NAME from YOUR realty firm. We are a direct-foreclosure-listing brokerage firm (REPLACE WITH YOUR VALUE ADD) and offer all our agents 100% commission. We're looking for one or two agents to work our exclusive inventory. What day works best for you to pass by our office to chat this week—Tuesday or Thursday?

Remember the unkept promises? Every agent wants these six items listed below, so switch out the script with your value proposition (fancy parties, car services, lavish office, etc.), and make sure you incorporate some of these hot buttons. For example, if you offer concierge service to all agents, switch out "direct-foreclosure-listing brokerage firm" with "Free Cadillac Escalade concierge service." The goal is to get them excited on the phone so they want more. Again, these six "unkept promises" are:

1. Branding and Technology
2. Support
3. Office Space
4. Trainings
5. Leads
6. Higher Commissions

Some agents will chat on the phone; some will hang up—but either way, it's all good. Your goal is to simply make appointments. If they object or are busy running around showing homes, say, "Okay, I'll set you up a tentative appointment and shoot you an email with the information." By using the noncommittal phrase "tentative appointment," you will get a 30% response rate. For those who don't show, you continue to send them automatic or "drip emails" in which you follow up with them weekly until they finally come in or say "no." When it comes to recruiting, you want to stay in the agent's mind. If they say "no," that means it's a no today, but *not indefinitely*.

Many sales books on the market say it takes a buyer saying "no" seven times before they say "yes." This is true with recruiting as well, except it's usually two or three times. Remember: you are offering a way for the agent to make more money at no costs. You are not taking money from them. Why would anyone want to turn that down? You are changing their lives and their families' lives with increased pay. This is how you need to think and come across on the phone.

I faced many situations in which an agent, for example, had issues with their current broker, or was about to write a huge contract for a million-dollar offer, remembered my 100% whisper being sprinkled into his ear, and called me two months after he flat-out said "no" three times. All it takes is for the broker or manager to "rub someone the wrong way" for them to make the switch. Again, it's all a numbers game. Here is an example of an older weekly scoreboard from 2013–2014 that we put up at the office every day for our recruiters:

Weekend* 10/24/2013	DAILY GOALS		WEEKLY RECRUITS		
Current Agent Count: 346	*Calls:* *200*	*Appts:* *7*	*Lead Source:* *Calls*	*Lead Source:* *Online*	*Lead Source:* *Agent Referrals*
MON	180	7	2	0	1
TUE	210	10	1	0	1
WED	170	8	1	1	0
THUR	205	5	3	0	0
FRI	185	9	1	0	0
Goal's End Date	12/31/13	3/31/14	6/30/14	9/30/14	12/31/14
Agent Count	440	480	520	560	600

*For the week ending on 10/24/2013 we recruited eight agents from phone calls, one from online searches, and two from current agent referrals, for a **grand total of 11 new agents!**

Every day our formula at the office was a set number of daily calls, daily appointments, and weekly recruits. The math worked like this based on our market, but was pretty standardized across different 100-percenters in various dense cities:

200 phone calls a day = 7–10 appointments a day = 8–10 recruits a week.

This was simply on outbound phone calls. As indicated in the chart above, online leads (agents who found us on search engines) or current agent referrals (current agents spreading the good word) can yield you about 20–30% or two to three extra agents a week. This formula per recruiter, when implemented in your office, will yield a brokerage 30–40 new agent recruits per month or, conservatively, 360 agents per year. Repeat this process for three years and you have:

360 agents a year x 36 months (3 years) = 1,080 agents!

Remember: this doesn't include the bonus agents that come from your online leads or your current agent referrals. I intentionally omitted those numbers to be extra-conservative, because you can't really control these variables. Conversely, what you can control are outbound phone calls. Now, I know I'm getting ahead of myself before the next chapter but:

1,080 agents x $795 a file x 30% that actually produce = $257,580 a month!

Yes, that is per month, not per year. This business is all about passive income because it's volume-driven. What's the "30% that actually produce" about? We will cover that in the next chapter, but it's basically the percentage of agents who actually close deals. This number has been consistent with me for the past ten years. That's why I emphasize going after volume. The more agents you get, the more money you will make. Now some opponents may be thinking about the astronomical amounts of risks (namely, complaints and agent-error lawsuits) that accompany these many transactions. These risks are real, but don't you think that making $250,000 a month (around $3 million a year) can buy you a lot of attorney hours, insurance, staff, and software to hedge that risk? Absolutely.

This formula also assumes that there is one recr
calls. You can certainly double up on recruiters makij
all day, sending email blasts, or focusing on the oth
ing methods, but if the number of agents is limited in your town,
one recruiter is sufficient. What about attrition? If some of you were
thinking about this, bravo. There's a 10% attrition rate—that's it.
Again, that has been consistent for me over the past ten years.

The great news about the 100% commission model is that rarely
do agents drop off. If they do, they do so because real-estate sales is
not for them, they found a "nine-to-five job," or they couldn't afford
the MLS fees. These were our top three reasons why agents left. This
assumes, of course, that you constantly fulfill all six unkept promises.
For example, if your agent tries to reach you and you offer them no
support, they will leave.

Hopefully I got you excited. I still get goosebumps seeing all
those deals going through the office—it's exciting. Compare this to a
top plastic surgeon who went through fifteen years of post-graduate
schooling. Let's say that he or she does rhinoplasties (i.e., nose jobs),
which are known to be worth about $5,000 a patient. To make an
equivalent of $3 million a year (the equivalent of what a broker with
500 agents would make using this model), he or she would have to
do 600 nose jobs a year (actually 30–40% more to cover the overhead, because this is a gross number).

Imagine all the nurses and staff that it would take to keep up to
that model. Not to mention the malpractice insurance—remember
that they are working on live human beings. Now, that is risky. Most
importantly, it's not passive income, as the surgeon is always ham-
mering away. Oh, did I mention that actually getting into medical
school, obtaining a medical degree, and being privileged enough to
get into a plastic surgery residency would set you up to potentially
make less than a 100% commission broker without a college degree?
Passive income is the only stream of income you should focus on.
Companies buy cash-flow streams, not management.

Okay, back to business. Who did we call? The two biggest sources of phone calls were competitor offices. Here is how we did it. We would sort through the MLS data and figure out which non-100% brokerages were within a five-mile radius. Remember, you want to locate your office in a heavily transactional price point for maximum turns (which are usually usually mid- to lower-price point). Why? If your office can "churn" out 50 transactions a month and you're making $795 a file, that's 50 x $795 = $39,750 in passive income. As you sleep, your agents are making you money, but they are making it for themselves as well. The amount of money they save by joining your firm is actually money they make. A dollar saved is a dollar earned, right?

Next, we would find the brokerages that had around 100 active listings in the MLS. This told me that the brokerage was not too small, but not too big either (in comparison, our firm had about 500 active listings during any given month). Sometimes smaller brokerages take it personally and you will get phone calls from their broker of record saying, "Stop recruiting me or I'll start recruiting you." I found this amusing, as the entire business of brokerage is based on sales and marketing. You're supposed to recruit and sell.

Besides, it's a free market. Anyone can jump in and set up shop tomorrow. Likewise, any agent has a right to switch to another brokerage company if they choose. Unless, of course, they sign a long-term contract, which is not customary in the business. The majority of the independent-contractor agreements between brokers and agents are open-ended: either party may terminate at any time for whatever reason.

So, my response would always be: "I would love for you to recruit our agents; however, it will be very unlikely because they are on 100% commission. Also, we give the same leads you do (it comes from the same companies discussed in the next chapter), and have a large office, live training, support, etc. In fact, how would you like to join your brokerage with ours?" Remember: always be closing!

Once you have identified each brokerage company, you want see who their top producers are. If a brokerage has 50 listings and they have 50 different listing agents, that tells you that they have 50 producers. However, realistically, you will see that a selected few agents (usually about 20%) account for a majority of their listings. So in this case, 10 agents make up for the bulk of the brokerage's listings (50 listings x 20% = 10 agents) and these are the "top producers" you want in your office.

Sometimes it's recruiting smart, not hard, but, again, with the 100% commission model, it's really casting a wide net and seeing what comes in. Many opponents of 100% commission say that cold-calling every licensed agent in town is "bottom-fishing" as these agents are not trained. This is not true. You are actually recruiting agents who have listings (i.e., producers). They are already trained to get listings, which is the most challenging aspect of the business. Therefore, call everyone in that office and once you bring a couple on board, you have leverage with the rest by saying, "You know Susie? Well, she just switched over."

Starting with the daily calls, our recruiters (paid hourly) would be required to make 200 calls a day. They then would be required to make a minimum of seven to ten appointments a day for the upcoming week. After an entire workweek, your calendar should have 50 tentative appointments for the week (10 a day x 5 business days = 50) x 4 weeks = 200 tentative appointments a month. This is at a minimum; depending on the momentum, we have made as many as 20 appointments in a day! Again, it's purely a numbers game. The more appointments you set means the more live interviews you have which equals the more agents that sign up.

While majority of appointments came from outbound calls, the other main sources of agent appointments came from: online and offline marketing (social media, direct mail, pay per click, Craigslist, etc.), and current agent referrals. Approximately 33% of our appointments were set using these methods. So, if 200 appointments came from outbound calls, we had approximately 100 appointments from these other "bonus" methods (if you can't quantify them the way you can with outbound calls, I called them "bonus").

Now, out of the 300 collective tentative appointments, our closing ratio was about 10–15%. After perfecting the system in our market, the maximum yield we got, after ironing out all the bugs, was that 15% of people who actually showed up, signed up. Some months were better and some were worse, but 30–45 new agents a month was right on target; slow and steady wins the cash-flow race!

**300 appointments x 15% = 45 new agents
signed up a month (max)**

Before each recruiter left the office, I wanted to know how many appointments were made, the names and numbers of the prospects, and the days and times when they were coming in. Why? Because I had to prepare to sign them up or "close" them. Once the agent stepped into the office there was a two-part system. First, our recruiter would bring them into their office and give a fifteen-minute value-add presentation highlighting why our unkept promises are in fact kept, and why it makes sense for them to keep more money in their pocket.

This is interesting. What we realized is that some people hate to be wrong. They will do anything to feel like they did not make a mistake. This usually starts off with "Yeah, but . . . ." This tells me they are saving face (and not really defending their current brokerage), especially if you can outmatch all of the six unkept promises. This is known as "effort justification" in social psychology. Facts and numbers don't lie. It makes sense to make the switch.

After that, our recruiter would give them a tour of the office and finally hand off the agent to me, as the principal broker to recruit, and then she would move on to the next appointment. We would always create appointment windows very close to be efficient, but mostly to create the impression that we were in demand (not that we weren't, but it's important to show it, rather than say it).

Once I greeted them I knew they were warmed up, excited, and ready to be signed up and join the firm. They just needed the final validation point to ensure they were making the right decision. Therefore, I went into my live closing checklist (see Appendix B). After doing this for so many years I had it down to a science: knowing what to say, figuring out their hot button, etc.

A lot of agents wanted different things. For example, some wanted more control than they could achieve at big box realty companies. They couldn't input their own listings, they had to get approval for any marginal change in design for advertising, and most importantly, they had to wait two or three weeks to be paid. As they pointed out, it was a "corporate job without the salary." We had a policy that stipulated that we pay each agent on the same day of the transaction via direct deposit into their bank account—an incredible value advantage. Some agents couldn't make the switch because their current brokers "kidnapped" their listings.

Many brokers would put sneaky clauses in their independent contractors' agreement stating that if the agent left for whatever reason (even though "there's no long-term commitment"), they would have to assign the file to another agent in the firm, even if it was ready, steady, and set to close. This meant that the agent would take a pay cut in their already low-paying commission split. It's dirty, but legal.

This really irked me. They do all the work to get the business and the broker holds them hostage until their deal closes, or else they only receive a 30% commission split versus 50%. In this scenario, we marked off the date when their last pending deal closed and we continued to follow up with them until that ribbon-cutting event. Once they signed up I handed them to our support/service personnel to assist in submitting the proper docs to officially transfer over, changing their MLS subscription to reflect our company (each listing in the MLS is assigned to a specific agent for a specific time), downloading our logos, creating yard signs, etc. It was a triangle offense, an assembly line; it was Chipotle.

RECRUITER
200 calls a day, 7-10 appointments
a day, 8-10 recruits a week

Closing Deals

BROKER
Always Be Closing! 30-45
recruits a month

Use Live Closing Checklist
(Appendix B)

SUPPORT/SERVICE
Orients new agent with
systems, contracts,
transferring over MLS, etc.

Although I emphasize calls as the number-one recruiting method, there are other ways that have worked as well, and I recommend doing them simultaneously. The first is targeted ads. Use Facebook and Google pay-per-click. Get all your ads made on www.fiverr.com (for five bucks you look like a rock star). Also hire people to do your search engine optimization (SEO). The minute someone types in "100% commission," you should pop up on page one or two on Google and Bing; this is the goal. You do this by purchasing 30–40 domain names that are similar to "100% commission," such as "100% real estate YOUR CITY" and create landing pages (one-page websites) to generate agent leads.

Don't worry if it sounds confusing; all this can be outsourced overseas very cheaply by placing ads on www.elance.com and other competing sites (see Appendix A). Everything is dependent upon budget, but allocate 10–15% of your revenue toward this. Your goal is to assist your recruiter with as many leads as possible.

Remember, on the scoreboard we had columns for 1) Calls, 2) Online, and 3) Referrals. Since our industry is extremely targeted, as discussed previously, you can use tons of email marketing companies, such as www.constantcontact.com, to email out your value propositions. I also posted free ads on Craigslist.com that worked wonders. You can check out my tried, tested, and proven recruiting ads in Appendix C.

Up to this point, we have talked about going after somewhat "seasoned" agents, those defined as having listings on the MLS. Another strategy is going after the "rookies" who just became licensed and know nothing about the business. This is the "sandbox" or playground for the big box realty franchises. The minute someone registers to take the state licensing test to become a real-estate sales associate, they probably have, on average, 10–15 flyers, mainly from the big players promoting mentorship or "training." So can you, except you can add in big, bold font:

100% COMMISSION + LIVE MENTORSHIP + NO MONTHLY FEE

Whatever a big box realty franchise can do, so can you, while giving more money back to the agent to improve their life. This is what I call a true "win-win" scenario. The mentorship plan works like this. Many 100-percenters have used this model very effectively. Once a rookie signs up, they can elect to be mentored by someone from your brokerage. This usually is a senior sales associate who has been around the block and has pretty much seen it all. What's in it for them?

We'll ensure that on the rookie's first deal the mentor will receive 30% (out of the 100% commission). So, the rookie is partnered up with the mentor, which gives the rookie an opportunity to ask all the questions in the world with a live one-on-one coach. Meanwhile, the mentor, or "team leader," gets to coach and receives free labor to assist with his or her personal inventory (listings, buyer leads, etc.).

The typical time period for the rookie to be assigned to a mentor is for the first deal or six months, whichever transpires first. Once the first deal closes, the mentor does not receive any more commission from the rookie. If the rookie cannot close a transaction within the six months, then the mentor is not obligated to use them anymore. Usually what happens is that both parties like their relationship so much that they decide to continue their arrangement past the six months, up until the rookie's first closing. Usually 180 days is customary for a first deal to close, but it depends on the rookie's sales ability. Building teams (naturally) within your large team of agents is always a good thing.

The next method of obtaining agents is through social media. You need to create awareness. Very few agents know about how much money they can save or earn by not giving it to their broker. Spread the word. Start with Instagram, Facebook, and Twitter. You must post one exciting event per day. You can use www.hootsuite.com and put up one post that can automatically post on all your social media. Examples of enticing posts that we had put up on a daily rotation were:

1. Live commission checks showing how much money the agent kept
2. Live trainings (i.e., weekly topics)
3. Exclusive listings off-market (or your special value add)
4. Motivational sales quotations
5. Open-invitation parties and happy hours
6. Funny videos of skits and comedy depicting the real-estate industry
7. Progress (show off major milestones, such as the signing of a new office lease)

Okay, blind posting is good but not great. To be a powerhouse marketer you must post with "hashtags." These are the "#" signs before the post, so in case anyone is searching for "100% commission" they type in "#100percentcommission" and guess who pops up first? Not your competitor. You do. For example, a sample post would be:

*Another agent making $3,000 and
keeping all of her commissions.*

*Call or email today to join.
#100percentcommission #100percentrealestate
#100% YOURCITY.*

The final big method of obtaining prospective agents, and my personal favorite, is current-agent referrals. Here is how it works. Each current agent of yours who signs up a brand new agent will receive $200 cash, for example, on that agent's first closing. So if your current agent brings on board five new agents who close purchase-and-sale deals, then that's an extra $1,000 in their pockets. Some agents are more excited about the $200 referral fee than the 100% commission. Why? Because they're going to tell everyone anyways about how their broker only took out $795 from their $15,000 commission, so they might as well get a thank-you bonus for doing so.

Here is what this is not—a big box realty multi-level marketing scheme. Many big box realty firms have a multi-level marketing gimmick that implies that agents are creating "passive income" from bringing others in under them. They promote this concept of "profit sharing" and residual income. This doesn't work and creates false expectations for most. Most agents who are "sold" on this sales pitch end up focusing on trying to make side money rather than on focusing on what's important—building their primary sales business. This eventually leads to frustration and cognitive dissonance.

They immediately look for another firm and hop around until they realize that real estate is not for them. Think about it: if the big box realty franchise is offering all its agents 50% net, they are keeping 50%. Out of the 50% they are giving you 10% off each agent you recruit, then maybe a pay-down for the next agent you bring in of 5%, then 2%, etc.

Everyone in this multi-level scheme is now forced to never receive

100% commission. The big box realty franchise further justifies this by saying that we cannot do so because we have to pay you a recruiting fee. It's a system that cannibalizes itself. It's repeating the same thing and expecting different results. It's insanity. Everyone deserves the maximum compensation. Being a real-estate agent or broker is hard work. Tons of deals don't close and there is a lot of running around every single day. It's only fair to get the maximum amount of pay, what the free market demands—100% commission.

Chapter 6
POINTS TO REMEMBER

» The secret to 1,000 agents in 36 months is to create an assembly line of service and support. From the recruiter bringing in leads, to the broker closing them, to the support staff getting them acquainted with the company. Think Chipotle!

» The five hottest ways to recruit real-estate agents are through calls or "dialing for dollars," online targeted ads and email blasts, direct mail to new licensees, social-media blasts, and current agent referrals.

» The recruiting formula is 200 calls a day = 7–10 appointments a day = 8–10 recruits a week = approximately 360 agents a year or 1,080 agents within 36 months.

» The potential of 1,080 agents at a $795 flat fee per file can make you more money than top plastic surgeons around the country: 1,080 agents x $795 a file x 30% that actually produce = $257,580 a month x 12 months = over $3 million a year in passive income! Making money while you sleep. No M.D. or sutures required.

» Social-media blasts with hashtags, creating 20–30 landing pages with different domain names, current agent referrals, and direct mail to rookies are some other ways that can be intertwined with outbound phone calls to get the maximum results when it comes to generating real-estate-agent leads for your recruiter.

7

Making Seven Streams of Income with 100% Commission

I've always said that a true millionaire has seven streams of income coming in at any given time. Rain or shine, deposits are pinging that bank account every single day. Many real-estate agents who do "luxury" sell three or four big deals a year. If they can touch $250,000 plus a year, they are ecstatic. The only problem is that they are then starving the next year and the vicious cycle continues—feast or famine.

As a 100% broker, you have seven main streams of income that you can potentially generate to smooth out any volatility in the marketplace such as: some agents dropping off, interest rates rising, and more competition entering. The seven streams are:

1. A flat fee per transaction, or monthly fees
2. Double-dipping transaction fees
3. Leads
4. Title
5. Mortgage
6. Commission Advances
7. Overrides

First is the conventional flat fee per transaction, or monthly fees. Different 100% commission brokers play around with either/or (and possibly both). From the marketplace I observed the average flat fee "all in" that a broker makes (i.e., including the E&O insurance and the transaction fee charged to the buyer or the seller) is around $595–$995. Some brokers don't want to wait for an agent's deal to close and trade off a higher all-in fee with a monthly membership plan. For example, pay $99 a month and your all-in fee is waived or reduced (e.g., $199). Many brokers in the 100% world offer three to five different monthly commission plans for agents such as "gold," "silver," and "platinum."

The general assumption is that most agents don't produce, and for you as a broker to be compensated for all the risk they take in the marketplace representing your brokerage, you should be paid something. What I realized in talking to thousands of agents during the recruiting process was that complicated means "no." Therefore, my pricing offering was really simple. One plan, one price, no monthly fee, if you don't close a deal you don't pay, no contracts. The agent has very little risk, which means every reason not to leave.

Besides, when times are tough, what is the first thing you cut off? Those monthly memberships and discretionary monthly-fee expenses. Let's do a quick hypothetical to see the two pricing models:

NO MONTHLY FEE

1,080 agents x $795 a file x 30% that actually produce

$257,580 a month passive

VS.

HYBRID MONTHLY FEE + LOW ALL-IN FEE

1,080 agents x $99 a month = $106,920 a month
+
1,080 agents x 30% that actually produce x $199 a file = $64,476 a month
_____

$106,920 + $64,476 = $171,396

As you can see, the "no monthly fee" approach is more lucrative and provides you with less attrition. If an agent has nothing to lose by keeping his or her license active and you are the lowest service provider in town (and fulfill the six unkept promises), why would they go anywhere? Conversely, you are trading off cash flow from day one. Remember: it takes time for agents to sign up with your firm, obtain listings, show homes, open escrow, battle out the contingencies, and actually close. A minimum ninety-day window at best. Test out your market and play with the numbers. At the end of the day the demand will speak. Just make sure that you are the number-one supplier.

The second stream of income that makes you a ton of money occurs when you double-dip the flat fees. Remember that almost all brokerages, 100% and non-100%, charge the real-estate agent's customer a "transaction fee" fee at the time of closing. Why? It's just another way to make money. It's pretty much a junk fee, but it's standard across the industry. Think of a "dealer fee" when you go buy a car. Every time your agent sells a home, you get this fee. Sometimes your agents end up representing both the seller and buyer, which is known as "double-dipping" a transaction. They make a six-percent commission (instead of the customary three percent), and you make an additional processing fee. It's dipping that crunchy, zesty chip back into the shared salsa bowl.

So, if your "all-in" fee to the agent was $300 flat fee + $100 for E&O insurance + $395 buyer transaction fee, for a total of $795, you actually made another $395 on the seller's side of the transaction. Therefore, $795 + $395 = $1,190 on a file. Wow! The likelihood of that occurring is around 15% of transactions, based on my sample size and ten years of experience. However, after consulting with many other 100% commission brokers, they would also agree.

One way to ensure that this happens is to spread your office listings around every week. For example, on every Friday we issued a hotsheet that displayed every single one of our agents' listings. Then, over the weekend, the magic happened. One agent showed another agent's listing, they worked on the file together, and everybody won: the listing agent, the selling agent, and the brokerage.

Next are leads, leads, and more leads! What agent doesn't scream for more? The number-one question I was asked daily was, "Do you provide leads?" The answer: absolutely. Here is how the game works. All leads come from the same place. Leads are buyers looking to buy a home and sellers looking to sell their home. Most brokers buy leads from online and farm them out on a round-robin rotation to their agents. The more agents produce, the more leads they get. The three biggest sources of leads are Realtor.com, Zillow.com, and Trulia.com.

Every time a potential homebuyer goes to these websites to search for their dream home, they end up signing in and putting in their search criteria. Within their search (e.g., zip code) certain listings or homes pop up. Once you click on a certain home you like, on the right side you will see either the "listing agent" who paid a premium to showcase his or her listing, or the "tell me more about this property" box, where you can request more information. This is, internally, the "lead."

Meanwhile brokers buy zip codes (e.g., 33156) from the same lead sources and all these potential homebuyer requests or leads are sold off in chunks to different brokers. Therefore, if my office is located in this specific zip code of 33156, I want to own that zip code to get all the potential homebuyer leads that inquire. However, Realtor.com is smart. They take that zip code and divide it into sections and sell you a piece of that section on a monthly plan. They then turn around and sell off the other piece to whomever else is willing to pay (i.e., your competitor). Therefore, there can be hundreds of brokers within a specific zip code buying leads.

The same goes with Zillow.com and Trulia.com. This also occurs with technology, as these companies sell the office solutions to manage agent files, transactions, contact management, agent websites, automated lead distribution, etc. One big player in this space is www.marketleader.com, a Trulia.com company. For leads and the technology, a broker can pay anywhere between $500 a month and $15,000 a month (or more), depending on how many leads and agents they want managed under their office.

Some brokers also get leads on their own through their own local advertising. For example, by placing ads in flyers, newspapers, and current listing signage they have around town. Imagine 500 agents and 30% of those with listings in your city. That is 150 homes with your office number and name on them, so when a potential homebuyer is driving around town, they call your office and you can capture that data as a "lead" and hand them off to your agents.

This was one of the biggest ways in which we captured leads. Representing the largest national banks, we were automatically syndicated to major foreclosure websites such as www.homepath.com or www.homesteps.com, where we would capture tons of potential buyer leads to distribute. Another way in which leads are captured is by "scraping data" from websites. You can hire computer programmers from www.elance.com to "scrape," or capture, all the data that are visible (e.g., email address, contact information, etc.) from the "housing wanted" section on www.craigslist.com, for example, to automatically be emailed out to you. So, every time a new person posts in the "housing wanted" section you are notified.

What you shouldn't do is post false advertising on craigslist.com to get phone calls. Many agents do this to get leads—especially rental leads (people looking to rent homes). They will post a building and a price but leave out the unit number to generate a phone call. Once they get the call, they say that the unit has just been sold or rented, but they have many others to show. This is unethical and you can be fined by your Realtor® ethics committee and lose your MLS privileges.

Now that you know where leads come from, it's time to learn how to make money from them. How we did it in our firm was to offer them on a 70/30 split. So if I spent the money advertising and bringing in a potential customer, I would offer a lead program for those that wanted it and they would be willing to pay the "house," or the brokerage, 30% for every deal that closed.

This, too, was a no-risk proposition for the agent because they got to work live buyers without paying for it (i.e., their going directly to Realtor.com and purchasing leads). The drawback with this was that some agents didn't take it seriously because they had nothing at stake and would burn valuable potential buyers. So, a customer relationship management (CRM) tracking software system (see Appendix A) was implemented to ensure proper follow-up. About 10% of the leads you hand out will close. That's it. This is because the lead quality is not good (buyers are not serious) or your agent doesn't work the lead correctly (e.g., takes too long to respond).

Therefore, you can also offer the leads on a flat-fee basis (e.g., $50 a lead) or a monthly-fee basis ($99 a month) for XYZ amount of leads. If you have enough bankroll, you can negotiate with the three biggest lead providers and get leads wholesale (at a cheaper rate) and sell them to your agents at retail (with a 40% markup). Test out the three different methods; they all work. In our firm we offered the leads on a 70/30 split with no other fees. Although it doesn't sound impressive, the numbers added up.

Assuming an average purchase price of $250,000 x 3% (your agent's commission) x 30% (house fee) = $2,250 per transaction. In the early years we were doing around 150 transactions a month x 12 months = 1,800 transactions a year x 10% success rate = 180 additional transactions. Now, multiply 180 deals a year x $2,250 per deal and you're talking about serious money = $405,000 a year bonus! We did have to subtract out the $5,000 a month in lead-generating expenses ($60,000), netting us $345,000 on the side. This is what we called "candy" in the business.

This also applies to rentals. Most agents work rentals in the beginning, as it's fast money. People rent houses in weeks, as opposed to looking to buy houses and actually closing, which can take months. If you can provide a stream of rental leads using the same methods outlined above, you can have faster turn of cash flow and recruit a lot of agents that specialize in rentals.

The fourth stream of income is in titles. Many big box realties and larger companies have in-house title services. I don't blame them; the numbers are incredible. Some states allow non-attorneys to hold escrow and sell title policies, but some states do not. If you are a broker in one of those states that does not, you may want to move to a state that does after seeing how much money title companies can make.

First, a word of precaution. Make sure that you have the proper licenses and affiliated business disclosure statements prepared and given to the consumer at the appropriate time in the sales cycle so you don't violate the Real Estate Settlement Procedures Act (RESPA); otherwise, you can be subject to criminal and civil penalties. You can visit United States Department of Housing and Urban Development website (hud.gov) to find out exactly what language you need in the disclosure. Okay, with that out of the way, let's talk about how title companies and brokers make money.

The brokerage company is the first point of contact with the homebuyer and the title company is the last. Once a real-estate agent prepares an offer, he or she sends that contract, along with the earnest money deposited to a title company or attorney (i.e., closing agent). This closing agent's job is to open up the file, hold funds in escrow, pull the preliminary title to see if there are any issues with the title that can prevent the sale, clear the title conditions (e.g., pay off outstanding violations and liens, obtain releases, etc.), manage the contract deadlines, adhere to lender protocol, prepare Housing and Urban Development's (HUD-1) settlement statement with all the appropriate figures for loan amounts, commissions, fees, etc., and finally issue the title policy.

Sounds like a lot. It is. It's arguably one of the most stressful facets of the real-estate brokerage cycle. Everyone is relying on you to close. Buyers have their deposits at risk after their inspection period expires, or they have their life belongings in a moving truck outside your office, sellers need their funds as they are about to close on another home, the real-estate agent is desperately in need of their commissions, the lender needs five more conditions cleared before sending the loan, the appraiser didn't find enough comparable to justify the value, and extensions are needed to buy more time. To top it all off, two years pass and a claim pops up on the title that prevents the home-buyer from refinancing or selling their home. So, to whom do they turn? You, the title company.

However, as the theory of risk and return states, the greater the risk, the greater the return. In the end, a closing agent's job is to sell. That's it. They are selling title insurance. If a deal closes, they get paid. If they didn't get paid, the deal didn't close. Although many buyers and sellers have the perception of title companies being more than that—it's not. Yes, they need staff to manage the timelines, but at the end of the day the closing agent needs to persuade the home-buyer to use them.

In fact, research "top title insurance companies" and you will see the same five names pop up in almost all of the lists based on market share: First American Title Insurance Company, Old Republic National Title Insurance Company, Chicago's Title Insurance Company, Fidelity National Title Insurance Company, and Stewart Title Guarantee Company.

So here is how title companies grow. They are considered a

business-to-business (B2B) vendor. They make their sales on soliciting real-estate firms to feed them business. On every closing, they make money in two ways:

1. Settlement fee: ranges from $395–$2,995 per side (buyer & seller)
2. Title insurance commission (buyer): typically 70% off the title policy shown on the HUD-1 settlement section. The actual title policy cost is regulated by each state by a promulgated rate.

Let's do some quick math. Assuming that you own your own title company as a broker and your office is doing 150 files a month x 30% that actually use your title company (you can't mandate it), that's 45 transactions a month. Let's assume that the average purchase price is $250,000 and the state-regulated rate is 0.005. Therefore, anyone who buys a home at $250,000 has to pay $250,000 x 0.005 = $1250 for a title policy. Let's also assume a $1,495 settlement fee to cover the costs of recording, copies, notary, FedEx, etc. Therefore the total gross profit on each file is $1,495 + $1,250 = $2,745.00.

45 title files x $2,745 x 12 months = $1,482,300!

These are real numbers. Okay, subtract out three full-time salaried personnel (a file opener, closer, and post-closer) at $60,000 a year x 3 = $180,000 in salary, and you are still netting over $1.3 million. Many of my associates who own title companies make one to three million dollars a year. Now instead of giving that money away to someone else, imagine keeping it in-house. Plus, imagine really marketing your firm as an all-in-one brokerage and getting that 30% conversion ratio up to 50% (with the proper disclosures, of course). Now we are talking serious money. This is how the professionals grow business.

Next, let's look at mortgage, which works in about the same

way. You can take about one or two percentage points off the loan amount for originating loans with the proper licenses and disclosures. This, however, is a lot harder to do today than it was before the housing crash of 2008. There are more regulations and many underwriters don't allow a broker's license and a mortgage license to be held by the same individual. However, the numbers work. Just one percent off of a loan issued for $250,000 is $2500 x 45 transactions a month x 30% that you can push in-house x 12 months = $405,000 extra! Nothing to roll your eyes over.

Commission advances and overrides are another feature of the brokerage that can yield you lots of small amounts of money at a fast pace. Here's what typically happens. As you start increasing your agent base you have more requests. Agents' deals get held up, they are counting on money that didn't come in because of a delay, and they are strapped for cash. They ask you if you are willing to advance them on their commission that is closing in two weeks. If it's a cash deal, and they have two or three other pending deals in the MLS (for collateral), and the title conditions are cleared, then you can make a nice 10–15% on your money in a very short period of time.

You can expect 10% of your agents to use this service. As long as you are a cheaper alternative than the check-cashing store or other real-estate commission advance offers, you will easily get the business. Why not? They are with your firm and under your supervision. It's an easy add-on sale that is a true win-win.

Next come overrides. Many agents need business cards, signs, lock boxes, etc. If you can negotiate a wholesale rate for all of your agents (cheaper than what they can get themselves), you have an opportunity to mark up your products. Again, make sure that it's cheaper than what they can get on their own, so it benefits everyone.

For example, 500 agents x a $20 mark-up on business cards = $10,000. Next, 500 lockboxes with a reasonable $10 mark-up = $5,000. Finally, 500 signs with a $15 mark-up = $7500. Sum up all three overrides and you are looking at an extra:

$10,000 business cards + $5,000 lockboxes
+ $7,500 signs = $22,500 a year!

The big picture is, once again, about creating value and a win-win scenario for yourself and your agents. Also, it's about volume. The minute you start growing, vendors will approach you to solicit your business. Many times I had free food, seminars, and trainings for my agents weekly by vendors hoping to get the business. Sometimes they did if the price was right. Sometimes they didn't. That's the name of the game. It's volume-driven at the end, so the more agents you have, the more money you can make.

Chapter 7
POINTS TO REMEMBER

» A true millionaire has seven streams of income pinging his or her account at any given time.

» The flat-fee commission model yields more profit than the monthly or hybrid models.

» In order to double-dip on the transaction fee to make more money, you should share your office listings with each agent via weekly email blasts and let them go to work.

» Leads can be an enormous profit potential when you offer them on a 70/30 split, monthly plan, or per lead basis. Obtain the leads from the top three sources, or on your own and hand them out with a CRM system to monitor them.

» Creating an in-house title company can make you one to three million dollars a year if, and only if, all proper affiliated business disclosures are given and rules are followed.

» The two major ways to make money owning your own title company are on the settlement fee ($395–$2,995) and the title policy commission (usually 70% of the premium paid by the customer).

» Mortgage origination can yield you one or two percent of the loan amount and is a nice way to make some extra cash, although the rules and regulations are harder than before.

» Commission advances and overrides are ways to make lots of small amounts of money at a fast pace. Mark up everything to your agents, but make sure it is still cheaper than what they could get on their own, so it's a true win-win scenario.

8

How Agents Can Double-Dip on Listing and Buyer Leads

The fastest way to grow your book of business as a real-estate agent is to get listings. This is the name of the game. Ask any veteran in the industry and he or she will tell you to focus on listings because they are cheaper to maintain, you get free advertising, it's less work, and it brings you more referral business around town. For example, when you sign an exclusive listing agreement with a seller (usually for six months), you have incredible marketing opportunities.

Signs on the front lawn, syndicated marketing through Realtor. com and various other websites, exclusive advertising without putting "courtesy of XYZ brokerage," and you get to double-dip on the transactions (i.e., make six percent versus the customary three percent). The smart buyers know to work with listing agents directly because they have a greater chance of getting their offer accepted in a hot real-estate market. The listing agent usually has the inside advantage because they know what offers are coming in on the home, and will usually pick their own customer whom they represent because they stand to make six percent over the three percent that they would working with another cooperating real-estate agent on the transaction.

Most importantly, it's less work. Put up a listing on the MLS, throw a lock box on the door, set up strict showing appointments, and let all the hardworking agents who are representing buyers' "selling agents" come to you. If your property is priced right, you have one hot house and three to five selling agents trying to sell your listing at any given time. Once you get one listing, you then turn around and prepare 6x9" or larger postcards and mail them out within a one-mile radius of the home, so every other homeowner knows that you are listing this house.

What happens? You start receiving calls from potential sellers interesting in finding out how much their home is worth, which turns into you obtaining their listing. Sooner or later, you control 30% of the market share in an area, have more control of your time, and get to double-dip on more transactions.

Conversely, working buyers is important, but requires more time with no guarantee. If you are on the other end of this scenario, you find buyers who have been working with you for three or four months, have narrowed down their choice to three houses within their budget, and who set up an appointment to look at their top choice or "dream home." As the customers fall in love with the house and you prepare the offer, the listing agent calls you saying, "Sorry, the home is pending contract." You just crushed your buyers' expectations and turned them off from the entire home-buying experience. What happened? The listing agent found their own buyer and made six percent by cutting you out of the deal.

Alternatively, you could have your offer accepted and, at the last minute, the lender calls and says that the underwriter didn't give the buyers a clear to close because they didn't meet their housing ratios. What? Exactly.

How about this? The buyer uses you to do the legwork (i.e., be the "Uber driver") and once you have narrowed down the top three homes, they use their licensed friend to write up the contract because they promised to give them a Home Depot™ gift card or some cash. Happens all the time.

Don't worry; there is a solution, and it is one of the biggest benefits of working with a 100% commission brokerage. The best way to retain and maximize or "double-dip" on your listing and buyer leads is to implement a cash-rebate model; offer a legal cash purchasing or selling rebate or credit towards closing costs. Since you, as an agent are keeping 100% of the pie less the house "all-in" fee, you have the opportunity to discount your commission back to the customer by as much as you want. Of course, make sure that it is legal in your state and get the proper RESPA disclosures, as discussed in chapter seven.

Think about it. If a consumer is in the market to buy a home and all the real-estate agents have access to the same home via the MLS, wouldn't they use you if you offered them 30 or 40% of your commission back, as opposed to a big box realty agent who simply gives them a box of fruit and a thank-you card? Absolutely. Do the math. $250,000 home x 3% = $7,500 in commission. Give the consumer 30% of that, which is a whopping $2,250 ($7500 x 30%) cash or credit towards closing costs. You are paying them to buy! Do you think they will try to circumvent you if their dream home gets sold? Not a chance.

You have a customer for life and they will tell everyone they know that you pay people to buy. In our firm, we have had agents, simply through word of mouth, triple their contact base by offering this. The best way to do this is spread the word online and offline. First, you need permission from your brokerage to do so. Most, if not all, 100-percenters actually encourage their agents to do so. Remember: all they want is their flat fee per file.

Assuming this is a go, blast it out everywhere, online and offline. Put it in your signature line, on your business cards, website, direct-mail blasts, and social media; tell everyone at networking events; let the whole world know you give out money. One great way to implement this is to visit all the development sites around town. Meet the inside sales reps for big-name developers such as Lennar, KB Homes,

Related Group, etc., and see if you can create an exclusive home-buyer program with them. Create flyers, do events, and promote it on social media with the end goal of creating awareness.

Many of my agents were allowed to set up booths and meet with at the development site with homebuyers who needed just a little more financial incentive to close on their dream home. Many times consumers walk straight into a developer unrepresented and do not have enough cash to close. If the inside sales rep has you in mind, they can refer that person to you and you can assist them with closing costs so a sale happens. Also, many times developers pay out big commissions (six to eight percent) to bring a buyer.

You can advertise this all over the Internet using the landing pages and SEO, as discussed in chapter six, to generate homebuyer leads. Once they call, tell them that you not only represent them for free, but you give back 30–40% of your commission in cash or towards their closing costs. Even by giving a commission rebate to your customer, you still make more money than a big box realty agent. It's a beautiful thing.

In fact, this model works so well that both Ziprealty.com (a publicly traded company, a ZIPR ticker) and Redfin.com advertise it nationally. Many of my agents used a rebate agreement to double their transactions (see Appendix D). Agents who went from zero sales, brand new in the business, touched over six figures within twelve months by paying people to buy.

The same goes with listings. If you can offer a one- or two-percent commission rebate to any seller who is willing to sell their home, that seller just saved a lot of money. Plus, you now have the opportunity, as an agent, to double-dip on the transaction. A typical listing pays out six-percent commission. Give a percentage point to both the listing side and the selling side (two percent) if you're representing both parties, and you are left with four percent. You can give more if you choose, as long as you make sure the brokerage company or "house" gets their fee.

The key to doubling your listing business is proper marketing after you get your first listing. This must run in conjunction with the cash-rebate model. What this doesn't mean is just "listing" it on the MLS and sitting back. One listing can generate you at least one other listing and one buyer, if it's priced right. Therefore, it's an incredible opportunity to share it with everyone. Some of my agents had lots of success with "For Sale" signs on the yard accompanied by "rider signs" that stated "$3,000 cash to buy."

Most calls are neighbors, curious to find out what's going on, which turns into a free "home value or appraisal," which then turns into you getting an appointment to list their home. Of course, replace the cash amount with whatever amount you are giving but make sure you take this approach and put it also in flyers and on your website, mail out free reports, mail out marketing statistical reports, put it on magnets, and, most importantly, your social media.

Also, a majority of times after you mail out a flyer within a one-mile radius of your current listing, known as the "farm area," prospective sellers will start calling you. These are the "warm-seller leads," and they give you an opportunity to meet with them in person to go over your discounted rebate plan to save them money on their home sale.

The most important and powerful listing method is a friendly phone call. Many MLS programs feature a tax-roll software that can allow you to obtain the phone numbers of residents within a certain area. If you can call them, make sure they are not on the National Do Not Call Registry (www.donotcall.gov), or any state do-not-call lists (there are tons of software products that can automate this for you, so Google it). Here is a great phone-call script to use to obtain a listing appointment:

Hi, this is YOUR NAME from YOUR COMPANY Realty. Did I catch you at a bad time? Great; we're just calling to let you know your neighbor's house just went up for sale and we are offering a cash rebate for anyone interested in buying it. If you happen to know anyone that is looking to buy or sell, please give them my name and number because this is an incredible opportunity."

Before you hang up, ask if you can email them a free home-value report with no obligation. Most of the time they will say "yes" and give you their email address. Once they do, you just built a new contact and the opportunity to stay in their minds when they are ready to list their homes. This cold-calling technique works great when you are offering free services and real value.

Thus, by implementing a cash-rebate model you have the ability to do what a traditional big box realty doesn't: pay people to buy and sell. Helping homebuyers with cash at closing or credit for closing costs can change their lives. However, a majority can't do this, due to their traditional real-estate commission structure, which is unfortunate. The good news is that it's never too late to be an agent of change, creating win-win scenarios and building customers for life.

Chapter 8
POINTS TO REMEMBER

» Focusing on listings is the key to accelerated growth. Savvy homebuyers go directly to listing agents to get their offers accepted. Plus, it's less work, and you have the ability to double-dip in commissions (and make 6% versus the customary 3%).

» Being a 100% commission agent allows you to implement a cash-rebate model. By sharing your commission with homebuyers, you can prevent them circumventing you and your being an "Uber driver," and you can close a lot more deals.

» The fastest way to hit six figures, if you are brand new in the business, is to network with inside sales reps from home developers and do a joint homebuyer rebate program. Many homebuyers need an extra incentive to close on their home, and you can be that agent ensuring that they obtain their dream home.

» By offering a one- to two-percent cash rebate or closing costs credit to a home seller, you can double your listings within a farm area, receive more prospect calls, and obtain direct-buyer leads, as they will be curious about the "cash to buy" incentive.

» Become an agent of change: change buyers' and sellers' lives by offering a cash rebate. Create win-win scenarios and you will build customers for life.

9

Final Thoughts for Agents, Brokers, and Buyers

new wave of real-estate brokerage has arrived. It's smart, it's
shrewd, it's fair, and it's competitive. It creates added value
for all stakeholders in the game: real-estate agents, brokers,
homebuyers, and investors. If you are an agent, by now you have
learned all the benefits of all the money you can save (or earn) by
switching to a 100% commission brokerage model. I'm not advocat-
ing doing so immediately, but simply keep an open mind.

Today the real-estate brokerage landscape has changed. With
the rapid advancement of technology, many brokers are offering similar training and other unkept promises that many big box realties
make. You work hard every day in the streets. You deserve every
penny from day one without being put up on a treadmill to "work
up to 100% commission."

If you are a broker (or thinking about being a broker), you have
the ability to offer 100% commission to all your agents. Follow the
principles laid out in this book and watch your business blossom.
The numbers are real. They work. You are creating a win-win scenario by giving more money back to your agent and, in return,
getting more volume and flat fees per transaction. Grow to 1000

agents within 36 months and shoot me a tweet once you get there. It's exciting!

If you are a homebuyer or investor, work with 100% commission agents. Remember that they all have access to the same houses on the market via the MLS. Plus, you get paid to buy and sell. Also, many 100-percenters today have grown so large and so fast that they can get you more exposure than can a traditional big box realty. Plus, they are more motivated to sell it fast: they are on 100% commission.

In the next decade, most, if not all brokerages, will adopt, in some fashion, the 100% commission model. It works. It gives money back and allows everyone to win.

This book's goal was to share with you what I discovered ten years ago that changed my life and the lives of all of my agents (and their customers). I strongly encourage everyone to adopt the 100% model in some way: the sooner, the better.

If you know anyone who is not maximizing their earning potential, share with them this model and pay it forward. It will pay dividends. I wish you an abundance of wealth and happiness. Be the best that you can be.

APPENDIX

A

Real-Estate Resources

The following are resources you will want to refer to in the trade to expand your business. Many services here are the exact ones I use. My criterion was that it either had to be free or at a very low cost. Like any other purchases, always get three estimates before making a purchasing decision. Enjoy.

Blogging

www.blogger.com
www.wordpress.com
www.movabletype.com
www.ezinearticles.com

Comparable Sales

www.zillow.com
www.eppraisal.com
www.propertyshark.com

Customer Relationship Management (CRM)

www.propertybase.com
www.realvolve.com

www.realtyjuggler.com
www.topproducer.com
www.wiseagent.com

Email Marketing

www.awebber.com
www.contact29.com
www.fabusend.com
www.fastemailflyers.com
www.happygrasshopper.com
www.icontact.com
www.mailchimp.com

Leads

www.marketleader.com
www.zillow.com
www.realtor.com

Lockboxes

www.padlocks4less.com
www.mfssupply.com
www.supraekey.com

Marketing

www.propertynut.com
www.trulia.com
www.listhub.com
www.postlets.com

Meetings & Conferences

www.go2meeting.com
www.freeconferencecall.com
www.skype.com

Notes & Doc Sharing

www.box.net
www.dropbox.com
www.gotomeeting.com
www.logmein.com
www.slideshare.net

Office Setup

www.toktumi.com
www.ooma.com
www.freedomvoice.com

www.grasshopper.com
www.rapidfax.com
www.davincivirtual.com
www.regus.com
www.intelligentoffice.com
www.adobe.com
www.gotomypc.com
www.carbonite.com

Projects (Staff-Hiring)

www.upwork.com
www.elance.com
www.craigslist.com
www.angieslist.com
www.fiverr.com

Real-Estate Agent Resources

www.realtor.com
www.redatum.com
www.terradatum.com
www.act.com
www.yardi.com
www.topproducer.com
www.ebrokerhouse.com

Real-Estate Agent Memberships

www.realtor.org
www.nareb.com
www.nahrep.org
www.areaa.org

Recruiting Software

www.mojosells.com
www.voicelogic.com
www.realtyjuggler.com
www.insidesales.com

Signs

www.buildasign.com
www.bigdaddyssigns.com
www.gotprint.com
www.signsonthecheap.com
www.real-post.com

Social Networking

www.activerain.com
www.hootsuite.com
www.linkedin.com
www.facebook.com
www.twitter.com
www.homethinking.com
www.instagram.com

Search Engine Optimization (SEO)

www.noblesamurai.com
www.seopowersuite.com

Used Office Furniture

www.arnoldsofficefurniture.com
www.craigslist.com

Website & Email Setup

www.alamode.com
www.godaddy.com
www.domainsbot.com
www.wordoid.com

Live-Agent Closing Script

1. **Build Rapport**: First, engage in small talk. Example: "Did you make it here okay? So tell me about yourself. How's business so far?" Next, give them two compliments about themselves. Example: "I like your watch/shoes or business cards (if they hand you one). Also, I noticed you just closed a big transaction. Congrats! (assuming you did some research on them before they came). Finally, find out if they have any pending sales. This is important because if they have pending sales at their current brokerage, they won't sign up instantly and by your knowing that, you can save yourself a good forty-five minutes on the interview. Don't kick them out, of course. Just go through this script faster and mark down in your calendar when their pending deals are completed, so that you can follow up.

2. **Identify Needs**: They either want 100% commission, leads, or exclusive inventory. What is their hot button? Your entire goal here is to identify what they want and why they took the time out of their day to sit with you. During the rapport process try to figure out what is really making them "itch"

to make the switch to you! It's usually going to be the 100% commission plan or your value advantage (leads, inventory, Cadillac Escalade service, etc.). Although they may like it all, there will be one main thing they want most from everything you have to offer. Once you figure that out, focus in on that throughout the rest of the interview.

3. **Present Solutions:** After you show them all the cool features at your brokerage, go over the sign-up packet with them page by page. Once that is complete, give them a brief summary: "So, look; in summary, we have 100% commission, zero monthly fees, support, you get paid the same day, exclusive inventory [YOUR VALUE ADVANTAGE], several offices, no contracts; if you don't like where you are, you can move your license tomorrow."

4. **Ask to Close:** If you want the sale, you have to ask for it! Ask the closing question (below), then stop talking. You need silence as it lets them gather their thoughts and make a decision (count to ten in your head and smile).

   a. **Direct Closing Questions:**
      i. I think you will be a great fit here and you will love it. I even have a small good-luck gift for you! Ready to get started?
      ii. Great; let's get started today. Do you have your license so I can make a copy?
      iii. Let's get started today; I have a great mentor who can show you the game. Do you have your license so I can make a copy?

A small "baby yes" will get them committed to signing on the spot. If they haven't committed, that means that they are still thinking about it. Therefore, you need to quickly obtain small commitments, "a baby yes," from them. Here's what you can ask:

b. Trial Closing Questions (If I can . . . will you?):

    i. If I can give you two or three cash buyer leads right now, will you call them today?

    ii. If I can give you two or three cash buyer leads right now, are you ready to get started today?

    iii. How many leads do you want to start with? Two or three?

    iv. Do you want your business cards delivered here or to your home?

    v. The minute you get a "baby yes" confirmation, go in for the close! "Great. Just start filling out this 100% sign-up packet while I assign you leads." Then hand them the pen, look down at the sign-up packet, and smile.

c. The Balance-Sheet Closing Question: Take a sheet of paper and draw a line down the middle so you can list your company's benefits versus their current company's benefits:

    i. For example, YOUR BROKERAGE vs. their 70/30 big box realty split, assuming a $250,000 purchase price x 3% = $7,500 − $795 FLAT FEE = $6,705 vs. $5,250 if they only kept 70% from the big box firm. Obviously it makes sense to make the switch.

    ii. You vs. Their Brokerage Comparison: List seven benefits of YOUR BROKERAGE and three benefits of theirs (after they tell you what's good about their current brokerage company) and say, "You see; we are a better option."

d. Hail-Mary Closing Question (if they say, "I'll think about it"): Don't give up; try these three as the last resort:

    i. What else can I do for to take the next step today?

    ii. What else can I do for you to start enjoying the benefits of our incredible 100% commission plan today?

    iii. Does that additional info make it easier to take the next step?

5. **The minute they join (i.e., sign up) go in for the "DOUBLE CLOSE":** Congrats, but you've got one more thing to sell them. You always want to close them twice. They are excited at this point and made a firm decision and believe in you and your brokerage. So get a referral. Strike when the iron is hot.

    Ask them, "Who else do you know that you can bring over? Please give me two or three names and numbers and I'll call them for you so you can get your $200 referral fee on their first closing."

Recruiting Ads

(These are to place on craigslist.com, online marketing, local papers, email blasts, newspapers, etc.)

Ad #1: Looking for Foreclosure Agents Ad (put your value add here)
Insert your company logo
ATTENTION all real-estate agents in [YOUR CITY, STATE.] We at [YOUR NAME] Realty are looking for one or two ambitious, hungry, motivated agents to work our exclusive inventory on 100% commission. All our agents earn 100% and only pay a flat fee of [YOUR PAYMENT PLAN] per transaction. No MONTHLY FEES EVER!

RIGHT NOW WE ARE IN A SELLER'S MARKET. Foreclosures will be flooding the market this year. We have tons of POCKET listings (PRE-MLS), and HOT buyers' leads. We only need one or two agents to help US WORK THE INVENTORY. Please call or email us today for more information: [YOUR NAME, BROKERAGE NAME, and PHONE NUMBER].

Ad #2: Numbers Don't Lie—100% Commission Facts Ad

Real-estate agents! If you are paying more than [YOUR PAYMENT PLAN] per transaction on your HARD-EARNED INCOME—stop! Numbers don't lie. Assuming you sell a nice single-family home for $300,000 and you earn three percent, which equals NINE THOUSAND DOLLARS. Why would you give up a penny more than [YOUR PAYMENT PLAN] per transaction? If you're giving up 30 PERCENT to your broker or franchise for doing NOTHING, THAT'S $2,700 DOWN THE DRAIN. At 20 PERCENT, that's $1,800 gone, poof, vanished. At 10 PERCENT that's $900 for what? Nothing! Make the switch today contact us for a confidential interview: [YOUR NAME, BROKERAGE NAME, and PHONE NUMBER].

Ad #3: 100% Commission Quick Benefits Ad

Join the fastest-growing 100% commission brokerage, [YOUR NAME] Realty, today. You deserve more money. Better pay. We have full support. Great training. We also pay you at closing. We have several offices throughout [YOUR CITY/STATE]. Check the scoreboard. Numbers don't lie. Call or email us today: [YOUR NAME, BROKERAGE NAME, and PHONE NUMBER].

Rebate Agreement

DISCLAIMER: PLEASE HAVE AN ATTORNEY PREPARE YOUR STATE-SPECIFIC REBATE AGREEMENT. THIS IS FOR EDUCATIONAL PURPOSES ONLY.

_____, Agent ("Agent") of YOUR COMPANY Realty, Broker ("YOUR COMPANY Realty") offers a rebate to his/her home-buying clients. A rebate is available only to buyers who close escrow/proceeds or final settlement with Agent of YOUR COMPANY Realty acting as his/her sole and exclusive Agent in the purchase of real estate. The rebate will be paid either in the form of a reduction of closing costs or by check, if approved, upon the successful close of escrow/settlement. Rebates are calculated as follows:

For the property listed below the rebate is **30%** of the cooperating broker commission actually received by the Agent of YOUR COMPANY Realty at the close of escrow/settlement, less a nominal $295.00 transaction fee. Occasionally, the seller and/or listing broker in a transaction will offer the broker representing the buyer a bonus or other additional incentive over and above the cooperating brokerage commission.

Any such bonus or other additional incentives are separate and apart from the cooperating brokerage commission actually received by the Agent of <u>YOUR COMPANY Realty</u>, and the buyer is not entitled to a rebate on any bonus or other additional incentive monies paid to the Agent of <u>YOUR COMPANY Realty</u> over and above the cooperating brokerage commission.

The amount of the cooperating broker commission received will vary for individual properties. The rebate will be paid or credited to the party or parties named as the "buyer(s)" or "borrower(s)" on the HUD-1 Closing Statement or equivalent official closing statement.

In the case of an IRC 1031 Tax Deferred Exchange ("Exchange"), the party named as the "buyer or borrower" is the Qualified Intermediary (the "Exchange Company") and the rebate will be paid or credited to the Exchange Company for the benefit of the party conducting the exchange (the "Exchanger"). All buyers, or in the case of any Exchange, the Exchanger must sign this Rebate Agreement before any rebate will be issued. This rebate program is only available where permitted under state and federal law and when not otherwise prohibited by the buyer's lender(s). <u>There may be tax consequences to the rebate. If you need legal or tax advice, you should consult with the appropriate professional.</u> Offer subject to conditions, limitations, exclusions, modifications, and/or discontinuation without notice.

I/We, the buyers(s) of the property referenced below, hereby instruct my/our Agent and/or **YOUR COMPANY Realty** to pay my/our rebate as **(circle): 1)** applicable towards my/our closing costs through escrow or **2)** a rebate check issued after close of escrow/final settlement. If this transaction is an Exchange, I/we understand that the rebate check will be issued to the Exchange Company.

Please mail checks or correspondence after the close of escrow/final settlement to the buyer(s) at the following **address:**

_____

_____

If this is an exchange, please provide the name and address of the Exchange Company, the Exchange Company Officer, and the Exchange Company file number: _____

I/We understand that my/our lender, Exchange Company or builder/developer (in the case of new home construction), may prohibit payment of this rebate. In that event, I/we have indicated my/our Agent and/or <u>YOUR COMPANY Realty</u> to make the payment in another manner allowed by my/our lender, Exchange Company, or builder/developer. In the event that my/our lender, Exchange Company or builder/developer prohibits, payment of the rebate completely, my/our Agent and/or <u>YOUR COMPANY Realty</u> shall not be obligated to make this rebate payment.

In no event shall I/we be entitled to a rebate that is prohibited by my/our lender, Exchange Company, builder/developer and/or local, state, or federal law.

Property Address:

_____

_____

_____   _____
Buyer's Signature   Date   Buyer's Signature   Date

_____   _____
Buyer's Printed Name   Date   Buyer's Printed Name   Date

_____   _____
Buyer's Social/Company EIN#   Buyer's Social/Company EIN#

<u>YOUR COMPANY Realty,</u> by   Date

About the Author

Aarambh "Aram" Shah is a serial entrepreneur, mentor, and consistent million-dollar producer. Aram started, built, and sold one of the largest 100% commission brokerage companies in the United States with over 500 real-estate agents. Aram is one of the early founders of the 100% commission model in the real-estate brokerage industry across North America. Aram also was a real-estate-owned property (REO) listing broker representing various banks throughout the United States. Aram holds a Master of Science degree in real-estate development (MSRED) from New York University Schack Institute of Real Estate, graduating top of his class and earning the honor "with distinction."

Aram has written two prior books within the real-estate industry: First was *REO Boom: How to Manage, List, and Cash in on Bank-Owned Properties*, an insider's guide for real-estate agents, which revealed the bestselling secrets on capitalizing off a down market during the great recession. The second is *The Art of Wholesaling Properties: How to Buy and Sell Real Estate without Cash or Credit*, which showed thousands of real-estate investors how to buy and sell real-estate contracts with little or nothing down.